ACTIVITIES FOR
TEACHING
PSYCHOLOGY
and LAW

ACTIVITIES FOR
TEACHING
PSYCHOLOGY
and LAW
A GUIDE FOR INSTRUCTORS

Amanda D. Zelechoski,
Melinda Wolbransky, and
Christina L. Riggs Romaine

AMERICAN PSYCHOLOGICAL ASSOCIATION
Washington, DC

The opinions and statements published are the responsibility of the authors, and such opinions and statements do not necessarily represent the policies of the American Psychological Association.

Published by
American Psychological Association
750 First Street, NE
Washington, DC 20002
www.apa.org

APA Order Department
P.O. Box 92984
Washington, DC 20090-2984
Phone: (800) 374-2721; Direct: (202) 336-5510
Fax: (202) 336-5502; TDD/TTY: (202) 336-6123
Online: http://www.apa.org/pubs/books
E-mail: order@apa.org

In the U.K., Europe, Africa, and the Middle East, copies may be ordered from
Eurospan Group
c/o Turpin Distribution
Pegasus Drive
Stratton Business Park
Biggleswade Bedfordshire
SG18 8TQ United Kingdom
Phone: +44 (0) 1767 604972
Fax: +44 (0) 1767 601640
Online: https://www.eurospanbookstore.com/apa
E-mail: eurospan@turpin-distribution.com

Typeset in Trump Mediaeval by Circle Graphics, Inc., Columbia, MD

Printer: Edwards Brothers Malloy, Ann Arbor, MI
Cover Designer: Naylor Design, Washington, DC

Library of Congress Cataloging-in-Publication Data
Names: Zelechoski, Amanda D., author. | Wolbransky, Melinda, author. | Riggs
    Romaine, Christina L., author.
Title: Activities for teaching psychology and law : a guide for instructors /
    Amanda D. Zelechoski, Melinda Wolbransky, and Christina L. Riggs Romaine.
Description: First edition. | Washington, DC : American Psychological
    Association, [2018] | Includes bibliographical references and index.
Identifiers: LCCN 2017040895| ISBN 9781433828898 | ISBN 1433828898
Subjects: LCSH: Forensic psychology--Study and teaching--United States. |
    Criminal justice, Administration of--Study and teaching--United States.
Classification: LCC RA1148 .Z45 2018 | DDC 614/.15076--dc23 LC record available at
https://lccn.loc.gov/2017040895

British Library Cataloguing-in-Publication Data
A CIP record is available from the British Library.

Printed in the United States of America
First Edition

http://dx.doi.org/10.1037/0000080-000

10 9 8 7 6 5 4 3 2 1

This book is dedicated to our current, former, and future students who inspire us to be more creative every day.

To Steve, Matt, Chris, and Jack, my biggest cheerleaders and toughest critics. Thanks for supporting me in writing my first "chapter book."
—*Amanda D. Zelechoski*

To my forever teachers, my parents Brenda and Steve, and my sister and best friend, Sarah.
—*Melinda Wolbransky*

To my teacher, Mr. George W. Granholt. Thanks and thanks and ever thanks.
—*Christina L. Riggs Romaine*

CONTENTS

PREFACE

This project started as many of the best projects do—over morning coffee at a conference, intermingled with sharing pictures from a child's recent birthday party and discussing holiday plans. The three of us have been close friends since graduate school and found ourselves teaching undergraduate psychology and law courses at three different institutions in the same semester. We started swapping ideas for experiential activities, and then the light bulb went on: We should use our classrooms as real-world laboratories to evaluate whether active participation in experiential exercises actually affects student performance in the area of psychology and law. We spent the next 2 years developing, implementing, and systematically evaluating various experiential learning activities in a controlled study and found that there was, indeed, a substantial return on our investment of time and energy into incorporating such activities.[1] Our students loved the activities, and our colleagues started asking us how to set up similar exercises in their classrooms. The next step seemed obvious: create even more activities and share them with fellow instructors in a user-friendly format. We hope you find this guide full of helpful ideas and suggestions in your efforts to inspire your students.

Speaking of inspiration, we want to acknowledge all those who have come before us in the fields of psychology and law and forensic psychology. Twenty years ago, this book may not have been possible. The rapid growth of our field and, by extension, the proliferation of psychology and law and related courses being offered is a testament to the field's pioneers and the generations of students and supervisees that have followed in their noble footsteps. We have had the privilege of learning from some of the best teachers, scholars, and practitioners in forensic psychology and hope that this book is a small step toward honoring those who have shaped our field and mentored countless rising students. We are particularly grateful to our mentor, Dr. Naomi Goldstein, who brought the three of us together in that little lab in Bellet all those years ago.

Similarly, we also want to acknowledge the American Psychology–Law Society (AP–LS), Division 41 of the American Psychological Association (APA), our professional and disciplinary home. AP–LS places a unique emphasis on teaching and training in the field and provides a great deal of support and resources to its teacher-scholar members. We are grateful for the encouragement and support we received for this book from many AP–LS members, as well as the Teaching, Training, and Careers Committee.

---

[1]Zelechoski, A. D., Riggs Romaine, C., & Wolbransky, M. (2017). Teaching psychology and law: An empirical evaluation of experiential learning. *Teaching of Psychology, 44*, 222–231. http://dx.doi.org/10.1177/0098628317711316

Next, we thank Dr. Kirk Heilbrun and Dr. Edie Greene, who provided ideas, advice, and encouragement every step of the way. Their dedication to creating accessible and engaging teaching resources in psychology and law was much of the inspiration for this project at its inception. We also thank Dr. Ashley Batastini for her participation as an instructor in the empirical study evaluating the effectiveness of the activities. We are ever grateful to Dr. David DeMatteo and Dr. Patricia Zapf for their guidance and sage advice as we navigated the book publishing process. Similarly, we want to thank Linda Malnasi McCarter, Beth Hatch, and everyone involved in the editorial and publication process at APA Books for their support and assistance throughout the writing of this book. Finally, we thank our students, who have been on this ride with us since the beginning, whether they knew it or not. They have been willing to try various iterations of these activities and provide honest and critical feedback, and we are deeply grateful that they trusted us to push them out of their comfort zones. Specifically, we are indebted to the following research assistants at Valparaiso University: Sarah Braun, Holly Buckman, Agata Freedle, Jaqueline Garcia, Olivia Gorman, Annaliise Hayrynen, Elizabeth Hostetler, Jared Joseph, Alexandra Katsahnias, Rose Leuhrs, Patrick MacDonnell, Samantha Schmidt, Christina Severino, and Kaylee Will; at John Jay College: Sofia Hamid and Clayton Santillo; and at Wheaton College: Heidi Brown, Kayla Cuadrado, Kate Gannon, Stephanie Jacobs, Kara-Jane Walker, and Moya Willis.

We would each also like to add a few personal acknowledgments.

Amanda D. Zelechoski: I would like to acknowledge my very first teachers, my mom and dad. Given what you were each most passionate about in your careers, I'm not sure how it never occurred to me that I'd end up being a teacher who focuses on legal issues in psychology. Go figure. Thank you for inspiring me and always encouraging me to be creative and dream bigger. I am also grateful to my siblings and their families and my extended Dovidio and Zelechoski families for their support and thoughtful inquiries throughout this writing process and my career. Next, I would like to acknowledge my Valparaiso University colleagues for their support and encouragement throughout this process. It is truly a privilege to be part of an institution that so deeply values and rewards exceptional teaching and mentoring. In addition, I want to express my gratitude to Mr. Ben Lieske, Valparaiso High School psychology teacher extraordinaire, and his students, who have been willing to partner with me many times to test out my latest activity idea. Finally, and most important, I thank Melinda and Christina, my partners in crime (pun intended). Thank you for keeping me on task and bringing me and my harebrained ideas back down to earth. Between us, we birthed multiple children, traveled the world, and started new jobs and life chapters over the course of this project. Working on this book with you has been one of the highlights of my career and I can't imagine having done it with anyone else. What a blessing you two are in my life. What should we do next?

Melinda Wolbransky: I would like to acknowledge my rich, worldwide support network of family, friends, colleagues, and, at times, even strangers. Portions of this book were written on three continents and in eight nations, bringing a truly global perspective to this work. Furthermore, none of this would have been possible without the many academic departments that have provided me the opportunity to teach their students. I especially want to express gratitude for the entire John Jay College of Criminal Justice Psychology Department, including Tom Kucharski and Angela Crossman, who opened the academic door for me. Last, I am most thankful for my coauthors, colleagues, and lifelong friends, Christina and Amanda. You two have inspired, encouraged, and shown me how to be a better person. I know that with you two in my corner, anything is possible. But seriously, what should we do next?

Christina L. Riggs Romaine: I am thankful to my parents—to Lee Riggs, for his unwavering faith and belief in me, and to Lynn Riggs, for teaching me to see the adventure at every turn and showing me what it means to be a teacher. Thank you to Dan Romaine, who has played every role in this project from tech support to test audience. He and my two tiny fierce ladies, Piper and Lola, make every day a joy. I have been blessed beyond measure. I am also thankful to have found an academic home at Wheaton College, in an amazing and collaborative department. It is an exceptional place to work and teach and I am very grateful. Special thanks to Chief Christopher Santiago of Wheaton Public Safety for bringing a nuanced and thoughtful law enforcement perspective to my classroom. Finally, although it risks repetition, I am ever thankful to my coauthors, coconspirators, and kindred spirits, Melinda and Amanda. It has been a joy to teach, research, and write together. I never knew 4-hour conference calls could be such fun. I am thankful for your friendship and wise counsel as we have navigated more than a decade together. As for what we do next, I have an idea . . .

ACTIVITIES FOR
TEACHING PSYCHOLOGY
and LAW

INTRODUCTION

You should use this book. Whether you are teaching a forensic psychology class for the first time, have been doing so for years, or are looking for ways to incorporate psychology and law material into a separate, yet related, course, you should use this book. Why? Because a body of empirical research supports the use of experiential and active learning techniques in the classroom. Specifically, the incorporation of these types of activities increases students' understanding of course material, their critical thinking skills, as well as their reported interest and motivation to learn content (e.g., Balch, 2012; Banyard & Fernald, 2002; Fass, 1999; Schwarzmueller, 2011).

As the number of courses offered in psychology and law and forensic psychology continues to rise, so does our understanding of what works in classrooms focused on psycholegal topics (Najdowski, Bottoms, Stevenson, & Veilleux, 2015). Several years ago, when we set out to systematically evaluate the effectiveness of incorporating experiential learning activities in undergraduate psychology and law courses, we were not sure what we would find. We knew that we, and many of our colleagues, enjoyed creating and implementing experiential learning opportunities in our courses and that our students seemed to thrive when presented with real-world simulations and tasks. But does it actually work? Does it improve learning in psychology and law courses?

As you may have guessed, it did (why else would we spend so much time writing this book?). In our study of just under 300 students across four universities, we found that including experiential activities increased exam performance for certain topics; it also consistently and significantly increased students' ratings of their interest and engagement in the course. Students rated the course and instructor higher when experiential activities were used and rated the coursework as more manageable (Zelechoski, Riggs

http://dx.doi.org/10.1037/0000080-001

Activities for Teaching Psychology and Law: A Guide for Instructors, by A. D. Zelechoski, M. Wolbransky, and C. L. Riggs Romaine

Romaine, & Wolbransky, 2017). Altogether, students in courses that used experiential activities were more engaged in the course and their learning. This is exactly what theory tells us should happen. Experiential learning engages students in an active learning process in which they are required to go beyond mere memorization, requiring a deeper level of evaluation, analysis, and application of course-related concepts. It demands students engage with the material, organizing it into meaningful concepts, and further comprehending under what conditions this information is useful (Bransford, Brown, & Cocking, 2000). Incorporating experiential activities in the classroom deepens student knowledge of core psycholegal concepts and improves student understanding of how to best apply this knowledge when faced with complex, real-world scenarios.

Accordingly, our goal was to create a collection of activities that apply to a wide range of topics typically covered in psychology and law, forensic psychology, and related courses. This book offers 17 experiential activities to enhance students' learning, understanding, and enjoyment of the related course content. The activities included in this book are not intended to serve as comprehensive coverage of all relevant topics or applications in the field of psychology and law. On the contrary, there are likely many more activities that can be considered, depending on the particular focus and scope of your course, the level of your students, and the logistical constraints you face in your setting. If you encounter topics you think are worth incorporating in experiential formats, please let us know.

AUDIENCE

The audience for this book is instructors who teach psychology and law-related topics in a wide variety of courses at various academic levels. For any activity, the depth and nuance introduced and required by the instructor can be varied to fit the course level. Our intent is that undergraduate faculty, law and graduate school professors, and even high school psychology teachers can find activities and ideas in this book to enhance their students' mastery and enjoyment of various content areas. We purposefully included activities related to a diverse array of topics that can be incorporated into a wide variety of psychology courses (e.g., forensic psychology, social psychology, cognitive psychology, introductory psychology, trauma psychology, developmental psychology, testing and assessment), as well as other disciplines (e.g., law, criminal justice, sociology, criminology, political science, social justice). This book does not assume you have particular expertise or experience as a forensic psychologist or attorney. Rather, every activity includes information about specific concepts and topics you will need to have covered in the course before facilitating the activity, as well as suggested print and electronic resources for you and your students to gain additional background knowledge, if needed or desired.

Many of the activities in this book have been tested in a variety of settings, including traditional, online, and hybrid class formats; small, medium, and large enrollment classes; and in high school, undergraduate, and graduate-level courses. Every activity includes suggested modifications for tailoring the activity to suit your particular class structure.

COMPANION WEBSITE

As you'll soon see, the activities in this book incorporate numerous class handouts. Some of the handouts are assignment sheets, and others are tools to assist in facilitating the activity. Each of these handouts can be modified depending on your course needs and logistics. Readers can download free electronic, modifiable versions of all handouts and grading rubrics from the book's companion website, http://pubs.apa.org/books/supp/zelechoski/. You are encouraged to modify these materials to best suit your class goals, content, structure, and practicalities. In addition, several activities require the use of visual or electronic media components (e.g., videos, pictures), which can also be accessed for free on the website.

Some of the activities focus on one specific topic in psychology and law (e.g., jury selection), and therefore, it would make sense to use them in class when that topic is being covered. However, other activities could be incorporated at various times throughout a psychology and law or forensic psychology course. Table 1 provides a quick overview of various topics for which each activity could apply, as well as the activity format(s) for traditional face-to-face courses. Each activity also includes modifications for online and hybrid courses, as well as classes of various sizes and lengths.

Each activity description is designed to provide all of the information you will need to effectively implement the activity within your course. Thus, each activity uses the following structure:

- *Overview:* This italicized section at the beginning of each activity gives a brief snapshot of the activity and how it might fit into your overall course format. We do not provide specific time lengths because each activity will vary with class size and depth of discussion and can be modified depending on the time you set aside for the activity.
- *Learning objectives:* This section provides specific learning goals you can modify depending on the extent to which you incorporate various elements of each activity.
- *Preparation:* This section explains what preparation is required before an activity can be effectively implemented. We offer a list of topics students should have learned, or, at a minimum, been introduced to, before engaging in the exercise. We also list the necessary materials for the activity, including handouts for you and/or the students (which can be accessed on the book's companion website).
- *Facilitation:* Step-by-step instructions are provided to help you smoothly implement the activity. These include tips for setting up the classroom, instructions to give to students, and suggestions for using the activity handouts.
- *Debriefing:* Once an activity has concluded, use the debriefing questions in this section to guide your class discussion after the activity is completed. This allows students to share their experiences, further apply the activity content to relevant course topics, and discuss any issues that arose during the exercise. Many consider this debriefing and reflection a central part of experiential learning (e.g., Kolb & Kolb, 2005) and you may find your students both enjoy and benefit from this reflection on what they experienced.
- *Grading:* Not every exercise needs to be formally evaluated or included in students' class grade calculations. However, many activities offer the opportunity to create a class requirement around that particular exercise and may serve as major course components (e.g., a final paper or group presentation). Specific grading rubrics have been included in Activities 10 and 16 because these are specialized writing assignments. Additionally, more general grading rubrics for participation, writing assignments, and class presentation are included in Appendixes A, B, and C and can be applied and modified for any activity depending on how you are using it within your course. Rubrics, like other activity materials, can also be found on the book's companion website.

doolittle

Table 1. *Overview of Activity Topics and Formats*

Activity	Topic areas	Format(s)
1. Fact or Fiction: Psychology and Law in the Media	Course introduction/overview	In-class activity
2. Legality Versus Morality Debate	Course introduction/overview Legal system Philosophies of justice and the basis for laws	In-class activity
3. A Brief Trial	Court process Legal system	In-class activity
4. Who Do You Want? The *Voir Dire* Process	Juries Jury selection research and evidence (Can be used as the start of a term-long mock-trial)	In-class activity
5. Psychological Profile of a Murder Suspect	Psychological component of criminal profiling Psychology of crime Theories of crime	In-class activity
6. Voices for Victims	Psychology of victimization Trauma in the justice system	Small-group presentations
7. To Protect and Serve: Training Law Enforcement	Police psychology Training and collaboration across disciplines and systems	Small-group presentations
8. Do You See What I See? Eyewitness Identification	Eyewitness memory False identification	In-class activity Writing assignment (optional)
9. To Waive or Not to Waive? *Miranda* Rights and Due Process	Interrogations *Miranda* rights and waivers Application of legal precedents	In-class activity
10. Evaluating Juvenile Competency to Stand Trial	Criminal forensic mental health assessment Juvenile justice Forensic report-writing	Writing assignment
11. A Journey Through Civil Commitment	Civil forensic mental health assessment Civil commitment	In-class activity Small-group presentations
12. Do You Swear to Tell the Truth? Expert Testimony	Expert witnesses/testimony Child custody	In-class activity
13. Can We Predict? Appraising and Reducing Risk	Sentencing Criminal forensic mental health assessment Risk assessment	Small-group presentations
14. Freeze! What's a Juvenile Justice Facility to Do?	Juvenile justice Forensic and clinical consulting	In-class activity
15. Problem Solved? Creating a Problem-Solving Court	Legal system Adult corrections	Small-group presentations
16. May It Please the Court: Amicus Curiae Brief	Public policy Legal system Court process	Writing assignment
17. What Would SCOTUS Do?	Trial process Judicial decision-making	In-class activity

- *Modifications:* Courses differ depending on the type of academic institution, student makeup (including varying majors), the term length (e.g., quarter, semester), or even the time of year. We offer suggestions on how the activity can fit into your class, regardless of how many students are enrolled, how many weeks are in a term, or how many hours per week your class meets. Furthermore, given the increase in hybrid and online courses being offered across the country, we include modifications for these class formats as well.
- *Content notes (for select activities):* Knowing that instructors will vary in their familiarity with any given topic, we include content notes for some activities. These provide basic background information about a topic when such information would be useful to you and your students.
- *Resources (for select activities)*: For some activities, we also include references to other sources for more information. Although the resource lists are not intended to be exhaustive, we believe they will help novice instructors or even students gain a better understanding of the topic.

HOW TO USE THIS BOOK

Choosing and Implementing Activities

It is probably not realistic to implement all of these activities in a semester-long course. Many of the activities require more than one class session, involve students working for a period of time in groups outside of the classroom, and demand different amounts of preparatory work. For these reasons, choose activities that best fit within your course. We suggest making this decision based on your individual teaching style, specific course goals, and a realistic evaluation of how much time you will need to effectively prepare, facilitate, and grade the activity (or activities). For each activity, we include information on the preparation required and the time students will need to reasonably complete the assignment. For example, Activity 16: May It Please the Court: Amicus Curiae Brief requires students to complete an independent review of the relevant literature and, as such, requires a period of several weeks between assignment and completion. It is important to note that these activities can be used in any class structure and with any relevant textbook. To help you decide when during the course an activity would be most beneficial, consult Table 1, which outlines the psychology and law topic(s) highlighted within each activity and lists the activity format. If you are incorporating more than one activity, varying the activity formats (e.g., in-class small-group discussions, out-of-class presentation preparation, a short writing assignment) may increase student interest and engagement.

We encourage you to read an activity all the way through (i.e., read the entire activity and take a look at the accompanying materials on the companion website) before deciding whether to implement it. This will ensure the smoothest implementation process. For each activity, you will want to set aside adequate time to cover the necessary didactic information beforehand. Some activities may only need part of a class; others take place over multiple class periods, requiring that you build in time for those sessions in your overall course schedule. Implementing these activities may also change your course grading structure, which is best decided before the start of a term (or as early as possible) so that it can be conveyed to students and any related questions or concerns addressed in a timely manner. We also encourage you to visit the book's companion website as you plan. For most of the activities, the resources posted there are key components for facilitation.

Creating Small Groups

Many of the activities consist of work undertaken in small groups (e.g., Activity 7: To Protect and Serve: Training Law Enforcement). There are differing opinions regarding how many students should work together for small-group activities. Some education scholars consider a small group as a minimum of three students because two students (otherwise referred to as a dyad) may not provide the diversity and creativity expected from small-group work (Beebe & Masterson, 2003). Others have cited six as the ideal number for small-group work (Booth, 1996), although a range from five to eight is viewed as acceptable (Exley & Dennick, 2004). That being said, as group size increases, the opportunity for each group member to actively participate decreases. It follows that the less time available for group work, the smaller the groups should be. There are also different benefits depending on the number of students in a small group. Smaller groups allow each member the opportunity to participate, provide more opportunity for physical proximity (increasing eye contact and other nonverbal communication), and greater feelings of responsibility to the group and other group members. At the upper range (five or six students), such groups provide a more diverse experience and more diverse viewpoints among members.

With regard to how to assign small groups, there are various options. You could choose to have students form their own groups. Typically, students will work together with those peers with whom they have a previous relationship (or friendship). This can result in groups in which students feel comfortable working with one another and implement effective communication styles. Conversely, students with prior friendships may not use time effectively. Other options for assigning groups include random selection (e.g., go around the room having students say "a," "b," "c," etc., and group accordingly) or creating groups based on known student characteristics. The last thing to consider is whether you will have students work in the same group throughout the term. This will depend on how many small-group activities you plan to include in a semester and on the class format. For example, we recommend that online classes keep small groups the same because it takes time for groups to develop effective communication strategies and learn each group member's role. Having the same group work together, therefore, allows for the best use of time.

Given this background, we suggest the following guidelines when implementing small-group work:

- Small groups should generally include between three and six students.
- Adjust the number of students in each group depending on your class size and goals for the group activity, attempting to make small groups of equal size.
- Be sure sufficient time is available for each group member to actively participate in the group (i.e., the less time available, the smaller the group size).
- Decide the method for choosing groups ahead of time, and consider using different methods if groups will change members between activities.

Setting the Stage

The last component to consider when implementing these experiential activities into your course is how to create the most realistic (i.e., "real-world") environment. In each activity, we offer practical considerations, such as how to set up your classroom furniture and what should be written on the whiteboard. There are also many activities in which you, as the instructor, may take on different roles and will want to portray that role accordingly (e.g., take a hard stance as a judge, ask challenging and confrontational questions as an attorney). As instructors using these activities, we have found it helpful to sometimes dress the part or otherwise visually demonstrate our changing roles to students. This can be as simple as standing on one side of the room when asking questions as the prosecuting attorney and on the other side when serving as the defense attorney, or as silly as holding a sign or image over one's head while serving in that role. Students have responded positively to these attempts and noted that they helped them understand the perspective and agenda of those in various roles.

Another easy way to increase an activity's ecological validity, or generalization to real-world settings, is to incorporate people who are actually involved in the focus of the activity. Collaborating with community partners provides numerous benefits to your students, the course, and possibly your work overall. We suggest you seek out the assistance of local attorneys, judges, police officers, or even high school students. Community members can play their respective roles in an activity. For example, an attorney can cross-examine students in Activity 12: Do You Swear to Tell the Truth? Expert Testimony. Alternatively, you could have high school students assume acting roles within an activity, such as playing the witnesses in Activity 5: Psychological Profile of a Murder Suspect. Even if they are not actively involved in the activity facilitation, asking a local police officer, campus security officer, or judge to attend a class on a relevant topic will provide students with a different and important perspective on how the exercise affects daily life and actual decision-making in various professions and roles. (For further discussion of these suggestions, see Zelechoski, 2016.)

Most important, have fun with these activities! As we have found, students who enjoy class are more motivated to learn the course content. The same is true for professors and instructors. We want to remain interested in the material we teach, including the methods we use to convey that information. In this way, we stay motivated and model for our students, through our creativity and enthusiasm, the importance of actively applying their knowledge throughout their academic and professional careers. We have found these activities to be effective in our classrooms and have had lots of fun writing, testing, and using them. We hope you will too. We are extremely interested in your implementation of these activities into your classrooms. We encourage you to tell us about your experiences, and are open, and excited, to hear your feedback (whatever that feedback might be!). We are always on the lookout for ways to further improve and empirically evaluate these activities or modifications thereof. We look forward to hearing from you.

RESOURCES   Baepler, P., Walker, J. D., Brooks, D. C., Saichaie, K., & Petersen, C. I. (2016). Managing student groups. In *A guide to teaching in the active learning classroom: History, Research, and Practice*. Sterling, VA: Stylus.

Jaques, D., & Salmon, G. (2008). *Learning in groups: A handbook for face-to-face and online environments* (4th ed.). New York, NY: Routledge.

Roberts, T. S., & McInnerney, J. M. (2007). Seven problems of online group learning (and their solutions). *Educational Technology & Society, 10*, 257–268. Retrieved from http://www.ifets.info/journals/10_4/22.pdf

REFERENCES

Balch, W. R. (2012). A free-recall demonstration versus a lecture-only control: Learning benefits. *Teaching of Psychology, 39*, 34–37. http://dx.doi.org/10.1177/0098628311430170

Banyard, V. L., & Fernald, P. S. (2002). Simulated family therapy: A classroom demonstration. *Teaching of Psychology, 29*, 223–226. http://dx.doi.org/10.1207/S15328023TOP2903_10

Beebe, S. A., & Masterson, J. T. (2003). *Communicating in small groups.* Boston, MA: Pearson Education.

Booth, A. (1996). Assessing group work. In A. Booth & P. Hyland (Eds.), *History in higher education* (pp. 276–297). Oxford, England: Blackwell.

Bransford, J. D., Brown, A. L., & Cocking, R. R. (Eds.). (2000). *How people learn: Brain, mind, experience, and school.* Washington, DC: National Academy Press.

Exley, K., & Dennick, R. (2004). *Small group teaching: Tutorials, seminars and beyond.* New York, NY: Routledge Falmer.

Fass, M. E. (1999). A forensic psychology exercise: Role-playing and the insanity defense. *Teaching of Psychology, 26*, 201–203. http://dx.doi.org/10.1207/S15328023TOP260309

Kolb, A., & Kolb, D. (2005). Learning styles and learning spaces: Enhancing experiential learning in higher education. *Academy of Management Learning & Education, 4*, 193–212. http://dx.doi.org/10.5465/AMLE.2005.17268566

Najdowski, C. J., Bottoms, B. L., Stevenson, M. C., & Veilleux, J. C. (2015). A historical review and resource guide to the scholarship of teaching and training in psychology and law and forensic psychology. *Training and Education in Professional Psychology, 9*, 217–228. http://dx.doi.org/10.1037/tep0000095

Schwarzmueller, A. (2011). A multi-model active learning experience for teaching social categorization. *Teaching of Psychology, 38*, 158–161. http://dx.doi.org/10.1177/0098628311411783

Zelechoski, A. D. (2016, Summer). Experiential learning in psychology and law. *American Psychology–Law Society Newsletter: Teaching Tips*, 10–12. Retrieved from http://www.apadivisions.org/division-41/publications/newsletters/news/2016/07/issue.pdf

Zelechoski, A. D., Riggs Romaine, C., & Wolbransky, M. (2017). Teaching psychology and law: An empirical evaluation of experiential learning. *Teaching of Psychology, 44*, 222–231. http://dx.doi.org/10.1177/0098628317711316

1 FACT OR FICTION: PSYCHOLOGY AND LAW IN THE MEDIA

This activity allows students to explore how the media portray psychologists and mental health professionals working in forensic settings, as well as their own perceptions of, and assumptions about, these various roles. By examining video clips and articles from both fictional (e.g., scripted television shows) and nonfictional (e.g., news) sources, students will examine the accuracies and misconceptions about the roles of mental health professionals in legal settings and be introduced broadly to the field of psychology and law.

LEARNING OBJECTIVES

Students will

(a) gain an understanding of the roles psychologists and mental health professionals play in legal settings,
(b) develop an ability to distinguish more and less accurate portrayals in the media,
(c) understand the scope of roles played by mental health professionals in forensic and legal settings, and
(d) identify at least three jobs or roles in psychology and law that were previously unknown or misunderstood.

PREPARATION

Prior Didactic Coverage

- This activity is designed to be part of the introduction to psychology and law and assumes no prior knowledge of the topic.
- Use this activity at the start of the semester before any class content is covered.
- The activity can be assigned before the first day of class. Alternatively, it can be assigned to be completed between the first and second class sessions for discussion during the second class meeting.

Materials Needed

- Handout 1.1: Psychology and Law in the Media Assignment Sheet
  ○ Edit to include when and how students should submit their materials. Electronic submission via e-mail or class website works well to allow students to submit video images, web links, and other electronic resources.
  ○ Choose a deadline that will allow you to review and compile the submissions before the class meeting in which Part 3 will occur.

http://dx.doi.org/10.1037/0000080-002
Activities for Teaching Psychology and Law: A Guide for Instructors, by A. D. Zelechoski, M. Wolbransky, and C. L. Riggs Romaine

As students are asked to locate and submit examples of media portrayals, a period of time (e.g., between class meetings) is needed between Part 1 and Part 3.

Part 1: Introduction and Assignment

- Introduce the assignment by briefly providing information about the rise in the popularity of "forensics" and the increased portrayal of psycholegal topics in the media in recent years. Depending on course format and timing of the assignment, you may choose to give this "introduction" in written form on a class website or via e-mail.
- Ask students if they are aware of any series or movies that portray professionals working at the intersection of psychology and law.
- Provide students with Handout 1.1 and clarify when and how they should submit their examples.
- Note that students are asked to find portrayals in both fictional and nonfiction media (at least one from each) and be sure to clarify the distinction to help facilitate this requirement.

Part 2: Compiling Submissions (instructor only)

- Review and compile submissions, grouping them into themes to discuss with students and preparing for discussion in Part 3.
- Within fictional submissions, look for ways to group or categorize the submitted materials (which may be photographs, articles, stories or video clips).
  ○ Separate submissions as accurate and inaccurate, common and uncommon (e.g., particularly around roles played by mental health professionals) or by domain (e.g., courtroom, evaluation, investigation).
  ○ Examples that are both accurate and inaccurate work particularly well for class discussion (e.g., a film clip showing a psychologist interviewing a defendant in a realistic-looking prison setting, but asking unrealistic, provocative, leading questions).
  ○ You can ask students to identify which aspects are more and less realistic. Students are often surprised by the adversarial and contentious style of questioning allowed during cross-examination, and illustrations of this process can be helpful.
- Within nonfiction submissions (often newspaper articles and clips from local news), it may be helpful to organize submissions by the context (e.g., mental health facility, evaluation, courtroom testimony, aiding police investigation) to discuss the diversity of contexts in which forensic professionals may work.
- Images and clips can be embedded into presentation slides for viewing and discussion in class.
- Begin with fiction clips (which tend to vary more widely in their accuracy) and then proceed to nonfiction clips.
- Depending on class size, you will likely be given more examples than can be reasonably discussed in class. Choose helpful or illustrative submissions. Not all submissions must be included. Make all submissions available on the class website, course management system, or other online platform, if possible.

Part 3: In-Class Discussion of Submissions

- Lead the class in a discussion of the various portrayals. View several submitted video clips and discuss the aspects that are more and less accurate and that are more and less probable for a practicing psychologist. Include consideration of the role of the mental health professional (e.g., as a profiler at the scene of a crime or conducting an interview), the setting, and how the professional goes about the task.
- For nonfiction clips, identify for students the exact role of the forensic mental health professional (e.g., trial consultant, expert witness, evaluator, fact witness).
- For all examples, when possible, preview for students how this topic will come up during the semester (e.g., for a clip of expert testimony, note that the class will learn about testimony and have the opportunity to serve as experts in an activity; see Activity 12 for expert witness–related activity).

DEBRIEFING   Lead the class in a brief discussion of the presented clips.

Sample Discussion Questions

- What roles surprised you?
- Overall, how accurate do you think media portrayal of psychology and law is?
- Was it difficult to find examples?
- Were certain types of examples more available than others?
- What inaccuracies were most surprising to you?
- Did you notice any themes in the inaccuracies portrayed?
- Has this activity made you particularly interested in any specific class topic?

GRADING   This activity will most likely be assessed generally as part of course participation. Students' submitted clips can be used as a record to give credit for participation. Grading should be based on each student's participation and engagement in the activity and his or her use of the available information. Appendix B: Participation Grading Rubric can be used and/or modified for this activity.

MODIFICATIONS   *Varying Class Lengths*

- This activity can easily be modified for use in any class length. You can vary the time spent as needed by limiting the number of examples shown.

Varying Class Sizes

- For large classes, consider modifying the instructions so that half of the class (e.g., last names with letters A–M) submits a fictional example and the other half a nonfiction example. This will reduce the number of examples for you to review and sort and will increase the likelihood students will see one of their submissions used in class (which, for many students, provides reinforcement for participation).

Online and/or Hybrid Courses

- This activity can be used online with little modification. Students may submit or post their contributions, and discussion can take place on a discussion board or other modality. You could select illustrative examples and create a presentation or post about the veracity of the various submissions.

RESOURCES   Roesch, R., & Zapf, P. A. (2016). Forensic psychology. In J. C. Norcross, G. R. VandenBos, & D. K. Freedheim (Eds.), *APA handbook of clinical psychology: Vol. 1. Roots and branches* (pp. 279–303). Washington, DC: American Psychological Association. http://dx.doi.org/10.1037/14772-014

Schwarzmueller, A. (2006). Critiquing media depictions of media professionals: A project for students. *Teaching of Psychology, 33,* 205–207.

Wargo, E. (2011, November). From the lab to the courtroom: How psychological scientists are having an impact on the legal system. *Observer, 24,* 10–14.

2 LEGALITY VERSUS MORALITY DEBATE

The legal system is said to be a reflection of society, where the laws are created to define what society believes is and is not acceptable behavior. Often, what we consider to be immoral is also illegal; however, the two do not always align. Certain laws criminalize behaviors people may actually believe to be moral—or at least moral "depending on the circumstances." This debate exercise highlights some of these conflicting views, engages students in critical thinking, and gives them an opportunity to work together early in the course. This activity can serve as a class introduction, as well as an icebreaker activity early on in the course.

LEARNING OBJECTIVES

Students will

(a) identify areas of potential conflict between what we or society believe to be moral behavior and what the law says is legal, or illegal, behavior;
(b) analyze an issue from a different perspective, thereby engaging in critical thinking;
(c) recognize some of the topics that will be covered throughout the course; and
(d) interact with classmates by preparing and communicating conflicting perspectives on a variety of topics.

PREPARATION

Prior Didactic Coverage

This activity can be used after discussing the often-conflicting views between the legal system and what society, or an individual, might consider to be moral behavior. It is expected to take one full class period to complete. Students would benefit from having a general understanding of the following terms and concepts:

- adversarial nature of the legal system,
- purpose of laws,
- defining legality and related challenges,
- defining morality, and
- inconsistencies between what the law says and what people feel or believe (e.g., euthanasia, abortion, death penalty).

http://dx.doi.org/10.1037/0000080-003
Activities for Teaching Psychology and Law: A Guide for Instructors, by A. D. Zelechoski, M. Wolbransky, and C. L. Riggs Romaine

Materials Needed

- Handout 2.1: Legality Versus Morality Debate Worksheet—Student Version (one copy for each student)
- Handout 2.2: Legality Versus Morality Debate Worksheet—Instructor Version
- Podiums or chairs and table set up to facilitate a debate
- Timer

FACILITATION

- *Activity as icebreaker:* Students may be more likely to engage in this classroom exercise early in the semester given the nature of the controversial topics. It is, therefore, a useful icebreaker activity. Although students may not view simple but "fun" icebreakers as meaningful (Henslee, Burgess, & Buskist, 2006), those that incorporate class content have been found to be beneficial (Anderson, McGuire, & Cory, 2011).
- *Alternative combined activity:* This activity could be combined with the activity described in Activity 3: A Brief Trial. Instead of using the scenarios in the form of a debate, they could be assigned as brief "trial" arguments to be made to a judge and jury. See Activity 3 for more details.

Before the Debate

1. Give an overview of the activity to the class, explaining the connection between the exercise and the topic of legality versus morality.
   - Students will be "debating" different issues that could be seen as moral, immoral, legal, or illegal. A list of these issues along with short descriptions will be submitted to the class. You are also provided with tips about how to assist the groups with understanding more abstract or less known issues from the list (see Handout 2.2). Debate topics include the use of psychological testing in releasing criminal offenders, parents' right to refuse medical treatment, criminalizing underage prostitution, parental monitoring in dependency cases, standing your ground, stealing to feed your child, legalizing marijuana, and regulating hate crimes.
   - It is also important to discuss the sensitivity of this exercise. Specifically, some of the topics are controversial, and it is likely many students already have personal views on some or all of the topics. Remind students to engage respectfully with each other, not to attack anyone personally, and to remain on the topic at hand. If a student feels strongly against participating given his or her personal views, decide how to best accommodate that in your class (e.g., he or she does not have to participate in the debate at all and/or can be assigned a different topic).
2. Set up "podiums" where the debate will take place. This can be two actual podiums or desks at the front of the room or two chairs at a table.

Facilitating the Debate

There are several options for how to facilitate this debate. The first and second options involve organizing small groups before the debate itself, allowing each group to prepare their arguments. The third option is a "rapid-fire" approach in which students are asked questions at the podium without any preparation time. Specific facilitation directions for each of the facilitation options are as follows:

Option 1: A Classic Debate

1. Divide class into groups of two or four students (depending on class size or how many different topics you would like to cover in the activity). Distribute Handout 2.1: Legality Versus Morality Debate Worksheet. Assign two groups the same topic from Handout 2.1, giving each group a different position. One group should be assigned to argue that the behavior described in the topic is moral, and therefore legal. The other group will argue the behavior is immoral, and therefore illegal.
2. Give groups time to develop their arguments and select one spokesperson (or, time permitting, divide up the arguments among group members) to argue their group's position in front of the class. If time allows, groups could be assigned during one class period and the debate held the following class period. This would allow groups more time to research and develop their respective arguments.
3. Choose the order of topics to be debated in front of the class. Allow 2 to 3 minutes for each group to present its initial argument. After both sides argue their chosen perspective, allow each side another 1 to 2 minutes to respond to the other side's argument. This should be modeled after a classic debate style activity.

Option 2: On-the-Spot Arguments for Both Sides

1. Divide class into groups of two or four students (depending on class size or how many different topics you would like to cover in the activity). Distribute Handout 2.1: Legality Versus Morality Debate Worksheet. Assign two groups the same topic from Handout 2.1, giving each group a different position. One group should be assigned to argue whether it believes the behavior described in the topic is moral or immoral. Members of the other group will argue whether they believe the behavior described in the topic is legal or illegal.
2. Give groups time to develop their arguments and select one spokesperson (or, time permitting, divide up the arguments among group members) to argue their group's position in front of the class. If time allows, groups could be assigned during one class period and the debate held the following class period. This would allow groups more time to research and develop their respective arguments.
3. Choose the order of topics to be debated in front of the class. Allow 2 to 3 minutes for each group to present its initial argument. After both sides argue their chosen perspective, ask them to make an argument for the opposite perspective (e.g., if a group argued a given behavior was legal, have those group members come up with a 1- to 2-minute argument, on the spot, for why that behavior is, in fact, illegal). Asking each side to make an argument from the opposite perspective can make for a good conversation about how to develop solid arguments, the importance of seeing your opponents' view, and the inherent challenges in deciding whether an issue is moral or immoral, legal or illegal.

Option 3: Rapid Fire

1. Have students come up two at a time to the podium or table. One student will be assigned to argue a behavior is moral and therefore legal, and the other student will be assigned to argue the behavior is immoral and therefore should be illegal. You may need to engage in a full class discussion before this happens to ensure that students have some familiarity with the possible issues presented and their potential implications.
2. Allow 2 to 3 minutes for each side's initial argument and a 1-minute rebuttal argument for each side. If there is time, this could be expanded to allow for 5-minute arguments and 2- to 3-minute rebuttals.

Regardless of which option you chose, engage in a full-class discussion between each topic about which perspective the groups chose, the different arguments made, additional arguments that could have been presented, and so on. You can also have the students vote on whether they would choose to legalize that behavior—in other words, after the debate, do the students view the behavior as needing to be classified as "illegal"? Is this belief consistent with their perspectives on whether the behavior is also "immoral"?

DEBRIEFING   At the end of the debate, debrief about the challenges between what we consider to be moral and/or legal behavior.

Sample Discussion Questions

- How do you feel about the notion that laws reflect society's views?
- Should some laws be flexible (e.g., debates may show that certain behaviors are considered moral or immoral depending on the circumstances)?
- If you are a lawmaker, how would you decide what is illegal when society disagrees about what is immoral?
- What did you learn about how to form a solid argument (e.g., the importance of thinking through the other sides' position(s) while forming your perspective's arguments)?
- What was challenging about forming your arguments?
- Were anyone's personal views affected by this exercise?

GRADING   Grading should be based on each student's participation and engagement in the activity and his or her use of the available information. Students should be given credit for attempts to engage in what may be unfamiliar topics and debate processes. Use of this activity early in the course can help students develop the skills of framing and making arguments. Depending on the course level, you may choose to evaluate the content, substance, or strength of arguments as appropriate. Appendix B: Participation Grading Rubric can be used and/or modified for this activity. (*Note.* You may need to grade differently depending on which facilitation option you chose for the activity.)

MODIFICATIONS   *Varying Class Lengths*

- If there is less in-class time for this activity, use a rapid-fire approach (Option 3), in which students are not given time to prepare their arguments.

- However, if more time is available, students can use time set aside to work together on developing their arguments, be given more time to argue each side (e.g., 5 minutes instead of 3), or more issues can be covered.

Varying Class Sizes

- Group size, as well as the number of issues assigned, will both depend on the number of students in the class.
- For smaller classes, this activity can work just as well as an individual activity instead of forming small groups. In this case, for Options 1 or 2, you would assign an issue to two students, each with a different perspective to argue.

Online and/or Hybrid Course

- Each of the topics could become its own online discussion around legality versus morality.
- Begin by reviewing the necessary didactic topics and highlight the often-conflicting views between morality versus legality. For hybrid classes, this preparatory discussion could be done in the classroom.
- Then, set up a discussion board or other online forum (e.g., a blog or wiki) for this activity. Present each topic from the list (or a chosen few). There are a few options for how to assign this activity:
  o Allow all students to engage in discussing whether the described behavior is immoral or moral—and therefore whether it follows that such behavior is illegal or legal. Explain the participation requirements to students beforehand and grade accordingly. For example, require students to post a certain number of times overall, a certain number of times for each topic, and/or a certain number of days throughout the week. Note that you will need to facilitate these discussions heavily to ensure students remain focused and that common challenges are brought to their attention. You may want to consider asking probing questions or raising issues that students are not discussing in the debate dialogue.
  o Assign students a topic and perspective, as is done in the formal classroom setting. Have students post their arguments in the appropriate location and allow the rest of the class to provide feedback and thoughts on the arguments made.
  o Students should be graded on their participation in both the initial argument and providing comments/feedback to others.
- To encourage discussion among students, require students (a) to reply to every comment made under or directly to their initial answers or arguments as well as (b) to answer any questions posed to them. Be sure to include this in the grading scheme or rubric.

REFERENCES

Anderson, D. M., McGuire, F. A., & Cory, L. (2011). The first day: It happens only once. *Teaching in Higher Education, 16,* 293–303. http://dx.doi.org/10.1080/13562517.2010.546526

Henslee, A., Burgess, D., & Buskist, W. (2006, Summer). Student preferences for first day of class activities. *Teaching of Psychology, 33,* 189–191.

3

A BRIEF TRIAL

Learning about and understanding the basic trial process provides students with an important foundation for any psychology and law or related course. Given the prevalence of television shows and movies depicting the trial process, many, if not most, students will have a basic understanding of the different parties involved and general trial process. This activity will allow students the opportunity to act out different trial roles and experience some of the more subtle differences between them.

LEARNING OBJECTIVES

Students will

(a) recognize the trial process and the different parties involved,
(b) apply knowledge of the nuances of serving various roles in a trial (e.g., attorney, judge, jury member),
(c) formulate and evaluate how attorneys develop arguments and how fact-finders make decisions, and
(d) compare and contrast the decision-making process of a judge versus a jury.

PREPARATION

Prior Didactic Coverage

- Basic trial process (e.g., opening arguments, direct vs. cross-examination)
- Different roles in the courtroom (including judge, jury, and attorneys)
- Similarities and differences between the judge and jury (and how each make decisions)

Materials Needed

- Handout 2.1: Legality Versus Morality Debate Worksheet—Student Version (one copy for each student)
- Handout 2.2: Legality Versus Morality Debate Worksheet—Instructor Version
- Courtroom setup: (a) podium for where attorneys will present arguments, (b) table and chair for the judge, and (c) enough chairs for each juror, grouped together in a "jury box"
- Timer (optional)

http://dx.doi.org/10.1037/0000080-004
Activities for Teaching Psychology and Law: A Guide for Instructors, by A. D. Zelechoski, M. Wolbransky, and C. L. Riggs Romaine

In this activity, students are assigned to play different roles in a trial (i.e., attorneys, judge, jury members). Using the dilemmas from Activity 2: Legality Versus Morality Debate, the attorneys will argue different sides of an issue to the assigned judge and jury members. Both fact-finders will then decide the case, as is done in a typical trial process. This will highlight the primary similarities, differences, and challenges presented to both the judge, as an independent decision-maker, and the jury, as a group of community members who must decide a case together.

Specific facilitation instructions are as follows:

1. Depending on how much prior preparation you would like students to complete, roles can be assigned on one day and the trial take place during a subsequent class period. Alternatively, roles can be assigned the same day the trial occurs, allowing for minimal preparation.
2. Give students a brief overview of the activity, explaining the connection between the exercise and a typical trial process (see Content Note 3.1).
   - *Alternate mock trial format:* Rather than a single class session activity, this activity could also be used as the start of a more comprehensive mock trial incorporated throughout the entire course term. Roles could be expanded to include both expert and fact witnesses, and students would have time throughout the term to research and develop their respective roles and arguments at various stages of the trial process (e.g., opening and closing arguments, direct and cross-examination).
3. Assign students to the following roles (*Note.* The number of students for each role will vary depending on class size and time allotted for the activity):
   - Attorney for each side
   - Judges
   - Jury (depending on the class size, juries can comprise six or 12 members)
4. Assign the different scenarios from Handout 2.1: Legality Versus Morality Debate Worksheet—Student Version to student attorneys, where one attorney must argue that the behavior is legal and the other that the behavior is illegal. (Note that in the Legality Versus Morality Debate activity, students are asked to argue legality as well as morality. We suggest assigning students to argue only the legality of the behaviors listed when using the current activity so as not to complicate or confuse the assignment.)
5. Provide student attorneys with time to prepare for making their arguments. The amount of time provided will likely vary depending on the amount of time you are able to devote to this activity. Instruct other students to meet with

Content Note 3.1. *Trial Process in the Real World*

- Explain to the class that this brief trial does have some differences from the typical trial process in the real world.
- Normally, both the judge and the jury are not deciding the same issues.
- If there is a jury, they are the final fact-finders and decision-makers, not the judge.
- If there is no jury (i.e., a bench trial), only the judge makes the final decision in the case.
- However, in order to highlight some similarities and differences between the two judicial processes, both the judge and jury will make final decisions in this brief mock trial activity.

their fellow "judges" or "juries," respectively, and generate ideas about how judges or juries typically make decisions.

6. After the preparation period, have students take their respective place within the mock courtroom setup.
7. Attorneys will each approach the podium and argue their side to the judge and jury. Set a time limit, if needed.
8. After each attorney argues his or her perspective, provide time for the judge and jury to consider and decide the case. Judges will need to act alone, whereas juries will need to come to a unanimous decision. To highlight these differences, ask judges (if multiple students are assigned) to reach a decision independently and prevent any conferring between judges. If time allows, have the "jury" experiment with different methods of decision-making (e.g., casting secret votes before discussion, discussing before votes are cast, secret ballot vs. open voting for a position, majority rule vs. unanimity).
9. Have each fact-finder render his or her decision/opinion to the whole class.
10. Repeat the mock trial process for each scenario assigned.

DEBRIEFING At the end of the mock trial, discuss the different courtroom roles and compare the decision-making process of the judge versus the jury.

Sample Discussion Questions

- How did this exercise affect your understanding of the trial process?
- What were the challenges of each role?
- What similarities do you see between the judge and jury?
- What differences do you see between the judge and jury?
- How did group dynamics affect the jury decision-making discussions?
- For those who played judges, how did you come to your decision?
- Were anyone's personal views affected by this exercise?

GRADING Grading should be based on each student's participation and engagement in the activity and his or her use of the available information. Use of this activity early in the course can help students to develop the skills of framing and making arguments. Depending on the level of the course, you may choose to evaluate the content, substance, or strength of arguments as appropriate. Appendix B: Participation Grading Rubric can be used and/or modified for this activity. If multiple experiential activities are used in the same term, make note of how each student participates in each activity. For example, students assigned to be attorneys may be asked to put forth more effort and greater preparation than students assigned to be judges. Be mindful of the potential disparity in workload, and for the next activity, be sure to vary student engagement and participation by assigning different students to more preparation-intense roles.

MODIFICATIONS *Varying Class Lengths*

If limited class time is available:

- Use one hypothetical scenario and one subsequent brief mock trial. A limitation to this modification is that not every student will participate in the activity;

therefore, it is even more important to ensure that every student is actively engaged in a discussion about the different concepts related to the activity, both before the trial begins and during the debriefing discussion.

- Limit the number of hypothetical scenarios/brief trials, while still engaging as many students as possible, by
  - having multiple students work together as attorneys (with only one or two making the final argument to the judge and jury); and/or
  - assigning multiple students to be judges and have multiple juries for the same scenario/brief trial.
- Consider limiting the amount of time attorneys have to argue their sides or limit the amount of time the judge and juries have to decide the case. To facilitate this, student attorneys could be instructed to prepare their arguments outside of class.

Varying Class Sizes

- The number of students assigned to each role and the number of scenarios/trials used will vary depending on class size.

Online and/or Hybrid Courses

- For hybrid classes in which students meet periodically in person, the activity can be facilitated in the same way as previously described. To reduce the amount of time needed in the brick-and-mortar classroom, the activity could be introduced and roles assigned in the online environment. This would also provide student attorneys time to prepare their arguments.
- Online classes will need to modify the activity setup. There are two options:
  - *Modification 1:* After the topics are discussed and the activity introduced, students can be assigned to one of the three roles the same as they would in the traditional classroom setting. However, instead of having the brief trial take place in real time, have student attorneys post their arguments to a specified discussion board for their trial topic. Assign a due date by which student judges and student juries need to post their rulings. If possible, provide juries with sufficient amount of time to discuss their rulings; this could be done within the classroom environment (in a specified discussion board), by requiring student juries to all be online or "live" at a certain time, or by asking them to set up a "meet" time outside of the online classroom so that they can discuss their decisions. After both the judge and jury post their rulings, debrief and discuss as previously laid out.
  - *Modification 2:* It may be difficult or too time-consuming to complete Modification 1. An alternative is to assign students a controversial issue and have each complete a written assignment. This written assignment could have three separate parts, and we suggest including the following instructions:
    1. Each trial has two parties arguing different sides of the given issue. Write a brief argument for each side of the issue assigned, one arguing that the issue is immoral and therefore should be illegal, and the other side arguing that the issue is moral and therefore should be legal.
    2. The trial fact-finder will listen to both perspectives and arguments made before deciding the case. In a jury trial, the jury is the ultimate decision-

maker. In a bench trial, the judge is the ultimate decision-maker. Think about how a judge would decide this case versus a jury. Answer the following questions:

a. What are the different ways a judge would analyze this case compared with a jury?

b. What similarities are there between the way a judge would analyze and decide this case compared with a jury?

c. What are the challenges a jury experiences when deciding a case?

3. State your final decision in this case and explain why and how you came to that decision.

RESOURCE   The Judicial Learning Center is an online resource with learning tools related to the court system (see http://judiciallearningcenter.org).

4 WHO DO YOU WANT? THE *Voir Dire* PROCESS

There are numerous theories about and methods for the process of selecting a jury. As part of the selection process, the decision-makers (both attorneys and the judge) must consider the legal rules and procedures, the facts of the case, and the demographics of each potential jury member. This activity is designed to provide students with a sense of the types of information judges and attorneys might consider when narrowing down the pool of potential jurors (the venire*) to the final jury. During this simulated* voir *dire process, students will also learn about the various legal challenges that can be raised by both parties during the jury selection process. This activity provides students with an opportunity to use critical thinking skills and gain exposure to difficult and sensitive topics commonly raised in the courtroom. This activity may also be used to establish a foundation for a larger mock trial implemented throughout the course.*

LEARNING OBJECTIVES

Students will

(a) gain an understanding of the purpose of *voir dire*;
(b) learn how general procedures, as well as how peremptory and challenges for cause, are used during *voir dire*;
(c) understand the purpose of a *Batson* challenge;
(d) exercise critical thinking in determining what information is relevant during the jury selection process; and
(e) demonstrate how the prosecution and/or defense use evidence from the case and juror characteristics to choose jurors.

PREPARATION

Prior Didactic Coverage

This activity should be incorporated after covering the topics of *voir dire* and jury selection through assigned readings, lectures, or other didactic formats. Most psychology and law textbooks will provide information on this process, and more information is available in texts written for both psychologists and attorneys (e.g., Kovera, 2013; Kovera & Cutler, 2013). Students should have a general understanding of the following terms and concepts prior to engaging in the activity:

- *venire* and *voir dire*;
- challenge for cause and peremptory challenge;
- *Batson* challenge (see Content Note 4.1);

http://dx.doi.org/10.1037/0000080-005
Activities for Teaching Psychology and Law: A Guide for Instructors, by A. D. Zelechoski, M. Wolbransky, and C. L. Riggs Romaine

Content Note 4.1. *What Is a Batson Challenge?*

In *Batson v. Kentucky* (1986), the Supreme Court of the United States decided it was unconstitutional to exclude jurors based on race. Therefore, in practice, if one attorney believes the other has based a peremptory challenge on race, they must raise that concern to the judge. This has been termed a "*Batson* challenge." The judge then asks for an explanation as to why that peremptory challenge was used, and a "race-neutral" explanation is often provided. On the basis of this explanation, the judge then decides whether the dismissal was in fact based on race. Challenging the peremptory challenge at the jury selection stage allows that party the right to appeal the entire case on the basis of this issue, if he or she later chooses to do so. This was extended to gender in *J.E.B. v. Alabama ex Rel TB* (1994).

- implicit bias and related theories;
  - To further expose students to the concept of implicit bias, you may want to have them complete an assessment of their own implicit bias either during or outside of class. An often-used implicit bias test that students can complete is the Implicit Association Test (IAT) through Harvard University (see https://implicit.harvard.edu/implicit).
- general jury-selection theories (e.g., similarity-leniency hypothesis, black sheep effect).

Materials Needed

- Handout 4.1: Simulated *Voir Dire* Process Activity Worksheet (one copy for each student)
- Handout 4.2: Juror Picture Cards, cut and separated (if possible, have cards laminated to allow for repeated use in future classes)
  - One small set for each group of three to six students
  - One additional larger set for the instructor
- Scotch or masking tape
- Dry erase marker or chalk, depending on classroom setup

FACILITATION   This activity can typically be completed in one class period. After didactic coverage of the jury selection process, the activity can be introduced and students prepared for the activity to take place the following class session.

Introduction

1. Briefly review terms and concepts listed in the Preparation section.
2. Explain to the students that they will be engaging in a mock jury selection, specifically the *voir dire* process. Half of the class will be prosecutors and the other half defense attorneys. A hypothetical alleged crime will be provided as well as descriptions and pictures of potential jury members.
3. You or someone knowledgeable about *voir dire* process should act as "judge."

Group Setup

1. Divide the class into groups of three to six students. Designate half of the groups as prosecution and half of the groups as defense counsel.

2. Provide each individual student with a copy of Handout 4.1.
3. Provide each group with one set of Juror Picture Cards.

Facilitation

1. Ask students to follow along on their worksheets while you read aloud the hypothetical case summary, as well as the specific court rules and procedures for this activity (e.g., number of peremptory challenges allowed). The case summary is as follows:

> Don Dillon is charged with first-degree burglary and attempted murder. The complaint alleges:
>
> Dillon broke into the Adams residence, 513 Third Avenue, City, State, at 1:00 a.m. on May 15. At the time, Mr. and Mrs. Adams, along with their three children, were sleeping in their respective bedrooms. Dillon broke the downstairs window, opened it, and entered the residence for the purpose of stealing electronic equipment and other valuables. While Dillon was inside the residence, Mr. Adams awoke and walked toward the kitchen. It was reported that upon seeing Mr. Adams, Dillon fired three shots with a 9mm Glock handgun. One of the three alleged shots hit Mr. Adams in the back, leaving him in critical condition (he will survive, but doctors report that he may be paralyzed). Upon hearing the commotion and before Dillon left the residence, Mrs. Adams and Ann Adams (the oldest of the three children) came into the hallway and witnessed Dillon leave from the same window he had used to enter the residence. All three witnesses gave descriptions of the perpetrator and assisted in the identification of Dillon upon arrest.
>   While in jail, Dillon was interviewed by local television reporters. During these interviews, Dillon claimed to be very sorry for what had occurred but denied that he had been the perpetrator of these crimes.

2. Each student should then take 5 to 10 minutes to read through each potential juror's description, with an eye toward his or her side of the case (i.e., prosecutor or defense). There are 20 potential jurors, and a description of each is provided in Handout 4.1 (available in full on the companion website). An example potential juror description is as follows:

> Sarah is a 29-year-old single woman of mixed ethnicity who lives in an expensive part of town. She is a journalist for a local magazine and frequently writes stories about local crime and how to keep the neighborhood safe.

3. After each student has read through the juror descriptions, instruct students to work together in small groups and *decide as a group* whether to keep each person on the jury.
   a. If they would like to ask the juror to be removed, they must determine whether they would like to use a challenge for cause (unlimited number) or peremptory challenge (two per side).
   b. If they use a challenge for cause, they must be prepared to adequately explain the reason(s) the juror would be inflexibly biased or unfair. They will need to argue these reasons to the "judge" accordingly.
   c. If they believe the other side will use a peremptory challenge, they are to think about the possibility of arguing a *Batson* challenge in response.

Figure 4.1. Jury box setup.

    d. Students should think critically about what additional information they would like to know about each of the jurors and include those questions on the worksheets. They will be allowed to ask a follow-up question of no more than three jurors during the overall class jury selection part of the exercise.

    e. See potential modifications for class size later in the activity.

Jury Box Setup

1. While the groups are wrapping up their discussions, prepare the Jury Box on the board as follows, by drawing the Jury Box on the left and taping up your complete set of individual juror cards. (See Figure 4.1.)
2. Once all of the student prosecutors and all of the student defense attorneys have agreed on their ideal juror selections, bring the class back together to complete the final step of the exercise: the *voir dire* process.

The Voir Dire *Process:*

1. Have all prosecutors sit on one half of the room and all defense attorneys on the other. The judge (whether this is you or a third party) should be at the front of the room.
2. Go through each potential juror one by one, pointing to that juror's picture and reading the description provided.
3. Allow each side to ask one follow-up question of up to three jurors.
    a. *Responding to juror follow-up questions:* You have flexibility as to how you would like to answer follow-up questions asked of particular jurors. If you (the instructor) are also playing the judge, then you can switch roles and play the juror to answer the follow-up question. If you have a third party playing the judge, then you (the instructor) can play each juror to whom follow-up questions are directed. For example, the prosecution might want to ask a particular juror whether she is opposed to the death penalty. The instructor would then respond to the question as she believes that juror would respond, based on that juror's description. You can also use this as an opportunity to incorporate additional jury selection topics that you deem important or relevant.

4. Ask whether either side (defense first, then prosecution) would like to challenge the potential juror.
   a. If neither side challenges, move the potential juror over to the Jury Box.
   b. If one side challenges for cause, they must state their reason(s). The judge then rules accordingly. There are two options for the judge when it comes to ruling on each potential juror when there has been a challenge for cause:
      i. sustaining the challenge will remove the juror, and
      ii. overruling the challenge will keep the person on the jury.
   c. If one side uses a peremptory challenge, see if the other side responds with a *Batson* challenge. If a *Batson* challenge is not used, remove the juror and keep track of how many peremptory challenges each side uses. If a *Batson* challenged is used, the procedure is as follows:
      i. Ask the side using the peremptory challenge to provide its reason for dismissing the juror.
      ii. If the reason given is race and gender neutral, overrule the *Batson* challenge and remove the potential juror.
      iii. If the reason is not race or gender neutral (which it always should be), do not remove (and be sure to engage in a more detailed discussion about this after the exercise).
5. The activity concludes when all of the potential jurors have been put forth. If more than 12 jurors are already in the Jury Box, then the remaining jurors who are not excluded can be placed below the Jury Box as juror alternates. If fewer than 12 jurors are in the Jury Box, then raise that as a point of discussion during the debriefing.

DEBRIEFING   After all potential jurors are discussed and the final jury has been selected, facilitate a debriefing discussion with the class.

Sample Discussion Questions

- What juror characteristics did all the prosecutor groups agree would make a juror inflexibly biased or unfair?
- What characteristics did defense groups agree would make a juror biased or unfair?
- In many cases, attorneys prefer to approach the bench to explain their reasons for wanting to remove a juror directly to the judge (instead of the whole courtroom). Why do you think this is the case?
- Why is it important to have an unlimited number of challenges for cause?
- What factors influenced your group's decision on when to use peremptory challenges?
- Was it easy or difficult to use a *Batson* challenge?
- Was it easy or difficult to overcome a *Batson* challenge?
- Why is it important to use a *Batson* challenge during this stage of the trial process?
- Did each prosecutor group choose the same jury? Why or why not?
- Did each defense attorney group choose the same jury? Why or why not?

Grading should be based on each student's participation and engagement in the activity and his or her use of the available information. Appendix B: Participation Grading Rubric can be used or modified for this activity.

Alternatively, or in addition, a written assignment can be incorporated and Appendix A: Written Assignment Grading Rubric modified and used, as appropriate. See modifications for online or hybrid courses in the next section for written assignment ideas.

MODIFICATIONS

Varying Class Lengths

- If class time is limited and it is not possible to provide didactic coverage of the jury selection process in a separate class session, dedicate an entire class session to jury selection by providing a minilecture on the *voir dire* process and how social science research has contributed to the process, followed immediately by facilitation of the activity.
- In this shortened format, carefully adjust the amount of time provided to students during each step of the project. For example, provide students with less time to work in small groups to determine who they would like to remain on the jury, or eliminate this step altogether.

Varying Class Sizes

- Adjust group sizes based on the number of students in the class.
- Depending on the size of the class and time constraints, you can also incorporate a second step of group consensus, in which you have all of the prosecution groups come together and all of the defense groups come together to try and reach over-all consensus regarding which jurors the prosecution would like to retain or remove and which jurors the defense would like to retain or remove. The goal is for all of the prosecutors to agree on their jurors and all of the defense attorneys to agree on theirs.
- Forming these larger groups will also provide students the opportunity to see that there can be multiple ways of choosing a jury. This is an excellent step if time allows. However, it can be challenging if the class is too large.
- For larger classes, if time permits, a second step can be incorporated in which two or three of the smaller groups come together in an attempt to reach another level of consensus (even if this means there are still multiple groups of prosecution and defense once the class comes together to engage in the final *voir dire* process).

Online and/or Hybrid Courses

- This activity is created for synchronous learning in which all students are engaged in the activity at the same time. Therefore, the small group deliberations and final *voir dire* process could take place in hybrid courses as previously described. The same may be true for online classes depending on the technology available.

- If synchronous learning is unavailable, modifications can be made. This activity can be assigned as small group or individual work as follows:
  1. Divide the class into small groups (or have students work on this individually).
  2. Assign which groups or students are prosecution or defense. Alternatively, you could have each group or individual look at the case from both the perspective of the prosecution and the defense. In a write-up, ask students to discuss the different characteristics and case details that were important to each side (i.e., compare and contrast what is important to each side and why).
  3. Post the juror pictures online so that they are available to all students.
  4. Have groups or students work through the deliberation phase and decide whether to keep each person on the jury.
  5. Create a discussion forum in which each group can post its final jury and explain why they asked each juror to be removed (i.e., challenge for cause and why or peremptory challenge). Students should be instructed to read each other's final jury selections and explanations and engage in discussions about what was similar or different between the final juries.
- You may choose to have students submit a written assignment for this project. This can be a description of the final jury and which challenges were used for whom and why, as well as a reflection component. Students can be asked to reflect on the questions posed under the preceding debriefing section (e.g., differences between prosecution and defense strategies, difficulties they might experience using *Batson* challenges, the importance of having unlimited challenges for cause).

RESOURCE

Greenwald, A. G., McGhee, D. E., & Schwartz, J. L. K. (1998). Measuring individual differences in implicit cognition: The Implicit Association Test. *Journal of Personality and Social Psychology, 74,* 1464–1480. http://dx.doi.org/10.1037/0022-3514.74.6.1464

REFERENCES

Batson v. Kentucky, 476 U.S. 79 (1986).

J.E.B. v. Alabama Ex Rel TB, 511 U.S. 127 (1994).

Kovera, M. B. (2013). Voir dire and jury selection. In R. K. Otto & I. B. Weiner (Eds.), *Handbook of psychology* (2nd ed., Vol. 11, pp. 630–647). New York, NY: Wiley.

Kovera, M. B., & Cutler, B. L. (2013). Evaluation for jury selection. In R. Roesch & P. A. Zapf (Eds.), *Forensic assessments in criminal and civil law: A handbook for lawyers* (pp. 88–102). New York, NY: Oxford University Press.

5 PSYCHOLOGICAL PROFILE OF A MURDER SUSPECT

The purpose of this activity is to introduce students to the process of integrating psychological science into aspects of criminal profiling, including what types of information are relevant when developing a criminal profile and what sources might provide such information. Students are asked to develop a psychological profile based on a criminal suspect. The activity provides students with a hypothetical crime scenario and then has them conduct interviews with various "informants" to gather relevant information about aspects of the suspect's background, recent behavior, patterns, and potential motives. Students then aggregate the information obtained to develop a comprehensive psychological profile.

LEARNING OBJECTIVES

Students will

    (a) collect and record relevant historical, psychological, and behavioral data about the suspect;

    (b) evaluate whether and to what extent various psychological factors likely played a role in the alleged crime;

    (c) compare and contrast the types of information provided by various informants;

    (d) formulate a cohesive psychological profile of the suspect; and

    (e) identify risks and benefits of conducting a psychological profile.

PREPARATION

Prior Didactic Coverage

- Theories of crime and why people commit crimes (e.g., biological, sociological, psychological theories)
- Process of criminal investigation, including how and when criminal profiling is used
- Patterns and types of offenders (e.g., violent–nonviolent; organized–disorganized; mass, spree, and serial killers)
- History, validity, and reliability of criminal profiling

Materials Needed

- Handout 5.1: Case Profiles (copied and cut for students assigned to each role)
- Handout 5.2: Informant Identification Placecards (one copy)
- Handout 5.3: Psychological Profile Worksheet (one copy for each student)
- Handout 5.4: Psychological Profile Report (one copy for each student)

http://dx.doi.org/10.1037/0000080-006
Activities for Teaching Psychology and Law: A Guide for Instructors, by A. D. Zelechoski, M. Wolbransky, and C. L. Riggs Romaine

- Depending on class size, you may choose to use either one or both case scenarios described in Handout 5.1.
- For each case scenario, have five students play the "informants" and the rest of the class work as profilers, either gathering data individually or in small groups of three to six students.
- For each case, provide the following instructions:
  - Instructions to informants:
    - You are going to play an informant, someone who knows the suspect or is involved in the investigation.
    - I will give you a few pieces of information about your character, which you will use to help answer the profilers' interview questions. You can expand your answers and descriptions about the suspect, but be sure to include the information provided.
  - Instructions to the remaining students:
    - I will read you the basic synopsis of the case. You will then interview the various informants, taking notes on your Psychological Profile Worksheet. Because you have to gather as much information from the informants as possible in a short period of time, make sure your questions are thoughtful and comprehensive.
    - At the end of the time allotted for data gathering, you will have time to work on your Psychological Profile Report (either individually or in small groups). At the end of the designated time period, we will discuss your respective psychological profiles (and/or you will submit your written profile reports to me).
- Read the case synopsis aloud to all students. (Note: You may want to change the names and genders of the roles if your class demographics do not allow for the roles as constructed.)

Case 1: Brian Benson

- Over the course of 4 weeks, a small rural town, Johnsonville, was terrorized by a series of unexplained brutal murders. Five teenage girls, all of whom were students at Johnsonville High School, were abducted while walking home from school and murdered within hours of their abduction. Their bodies were discovered in a forest about 10 miles from the high school. The suspect, Brian Benson, is a senior at Johnsonville High School.
- Roles: (a) Brian Benson (suspect), (b) Sgt. Perkins (police detective), (c) Ms. Benson (suspect's mother), (d) Ms. Smith (suspect's homeroom teacher), and (e) Ron Larson (suspect's best friend)

Case 2: Jason Jones

- Several days ago, Jason Jones, an employee of a large, well-known financial services firm, barged into his office and opened fire in the central office cubicle area, killing 10 people and wounding many others. He was quickly apprehended by multiple building security officers and was taken into custody shortly thereafter.

- Roles: (a) Jason Jones (suspect), (b) Sgt. Evans (police detective), (c) Pam Jones (suspect's estranged wife), (d) David Scott (suspect's boss), and (e) Bill Murphy (suspect's coworker)

- After the designated time to interview informants, provide time for students to synthesize the data gathered and prepare their psychological profile reports. You may choose to have them do this individually or in small groups. Small groups have the advantage of allowing students to put together all of their individual information and aggregate their collective knowledge into an overall profile. Conversely, having students prepare their reports individually allows you to demonstrate the wide variability in the type of data obtained and how it was interpreted by each student.
- Time permitting, have students report to the class their final psychological profiles and facilitate a discussion about the similarities and differences in the profiles. Alternatively, collect and grade the written psychological profile reports.
- Repeat these instructions for the second case, if desired and time permitting. This allows the students who played informants in the first case to have an opportunity to be profilers.
- Optional time breakdowns for this activity are as follows:
  - 50-minute class—Case 1 only:
    - 5 minutes: introduce the activity and brief the informants on their roles
    - 20 minutes: informant interviews
    - 15 minutes: develop integrated psychological profile (individually or in small groups)
    - 10 minutes: present final psychological profiles and debriefing discussion
  - 50-minute class—Case 1 and Case 2:
    - 5 to 10 minutes: introduce the activity, explain the writing assignment, and choose different informants for both cases so that every student has the opportunity to be a profiler
    - 20 minutes: Case 1 informant interviews
    - 20 minutes: Case 2 informant interviews
    - Remind students when written profile is due. Debrief at the start of next class or when students submit written profile.

DEBRIEFING

Lead a brief discussion about the process of interviewing informants and compiling their profiles.

Sample Discussion Questions

- What types of attributes are necessary for a successful criminal profiler (e.g., more experience with psychology, criminal investigation, or both)?
- To what extent should the criminal profiling process be considered scientifically reliable or valid?
- How do individual factors (e.g., gender, age, ethnicity, mental illness) fit into the bigger picture of a profile? What risks may emerge when putting weight on these individual factors?
- What are the pros and cons to creating a profile to attempt to predict the criminal's identity?

■ What was most challenging in this process? Was there other information you would want to have access to if forming a real profile?

GRADING   If students are required to submit a final psychological profile report, Appendix A: Written Assignment Grading Rubric can be modified as appropriate. Alternatively, or in addition, grading can be based on each student's participation and engagement in the activity and his or her use of the available information. Appendix B: Participation Grading Rubric can be used or modified for that purpose.

MODIFICATIONS   *Varying Class Lengths*

■ If you have a shorter class period (e.g., 50 minutes), you will likely only be able to get through one case, with some students serving as informants and the rest of the students working in small groups or individually as profilers. Even with only one case, it will require careful time management for each stage of the activity because each informant has a significant amount of information to convey.
■ If you have a longer class period (e.g., 75 minutes or longer) or can spread the activity over several class sessions, you are more likely to get through both case scenarios, allowing all students to serve as profilers at least once.
■ Alternatively, doing only one case scenario and allowing for a lengthier discussion segment at the end of the activity, in which students compare and contrast the findings in their profiles and talk through several debriefing questions, is likely more beneficial than trying to force a second case scenario into a limited time frame.

Varying Class Sizes

■ For larger classes (or shorter class periods), have the five informants sit in a panel at the front of the class. The rest of the students (either individually or arranged in small groups) can take turns asking the informants interview questions, allowing all students to hear the responses. After the designated interview period, students can then come together in their small groups to synthesize the information and develop a profile or do so individually. Alternatively, and if feasible given classroom layout, put each informant in a different part of the room and have the small groups rotate around to each informant for a set period of time (analogous to a speed-dating timed rotation).

Online and/or Hybrid Courses

■ Instead of having students role-play informants, tell students to presume they have already conducted interviews with each informant and post a document that summarizes their notes from the interviews. You can then slightly modify Handout 5.1: Case Scenarios and Roles and post it on your online platform, along with Handouts 5.3 and 5.4.
■ You can also decide whether you want to require students to develop a profile based only on the information reflected in their "notes" from each informant

interview or allow students to go beyond and extrapolate additional information (i.e., make up additional facts and details from each informant) to inform their profiles.

RESOURCES Greene, E., & Heilbrun, K. (2013). Evaluating criminal suspects. In *Wrightsman's psychology and the legal system* (8th ed., pp. 146–173). Belmont, CA: Wadsworth/ Cengage Learning.

Winerman, L. (2004). Criminal profiling: The reality behind the myth. *APA Monitor, 35,* 66. Retrieved from http://www.apa.org/monitor/julaug04/criminal.aspx

6 VOICES FOR VICTIMS

An important component of studying the criminal justice system is an understanding of victims and victimization. This includes understanding trends and circumstances related to frequently victimized groups, as well as societal perceptions of victims. It is also important to recognize the significant overlap between victims and perpetrators of crime. This activity is intended to provide students with an opportunity to work together to consider the needs and challenges of various victim groups, including unpopular victim groups, and engage in creating an advocacy initiative on behalf of that group.

LEARNING OBJECTIVES

Students will

(a) collaborate with peers to prepare an oral and written presentation of their advocacy initiative,
(b) identify issues and challenges faced by various types of victims,
(c) integrate information learned in the course and through outside research to design a victim advocacy initiative, and
(d) translate knowledge into creative and accessible presentation formats for consumers or the public.

PREPARATION

Prior Didactic Coverage

- Types of victims (e.g., child victims, adult victims)
- Types of crimes (e.g., violent, nonviolent, victimless)
- Offenders as victims (e.g., the significant prevalence of prior victimization of offenders)
- Revictimization (e.g., the increased likelihood of being repeatedly victimized, once you have been victimized once)
- Trends in societal perceptions of specific victim groups (e.g., rape and sexual assault victims, battered spouses)
- Who is a victim (i.e., why might we consider some groups to be victims, such as police officers)

http://dx.doi.org/10.1037/0000080-007
Activities for Teaching Psychology and Law: A Guide for Instructors, by A. D. Zelechoski, M. Wolbransky, and C. L. Riggs Romaine

Materials Needed

- Handout 6.1: Student Instructions (one copy for each student)
- Handout 6.2: Victim Groups (cut into strips to draw from a hat)
- Handout 6.3: Advocacy Initiatives (cut into strips to draw from a hat)

FACILITATION   *Preparatory Class Session*

- The timing of this preparatory class session will depend on the time allotted for students to design and prepare their advocacy initiatives. For example, this activity can be a substantial component of the course and comprise a significant portion of the students' overall grades. In that case, consider introducing the activity and assigning groups several weeks in advance of the due date. To use this activity as a small class component, without in-depth research or extensive preparation, introducing the task and assigning groups 1 week in advance is sufficient for students to be creative and engage in their design process.
- During the preparatory class session, divide the class into small groups (e.g., three to six students per group). There are different ways to consider creating groups, depending on whether you want students to select their victim groups or advocacy initiatives or to randomly assign these components. For example, you could (a) let students choose groups, (b) randomly assign groups, or (c) let students identify their top three choices of victim group and match them based on victim group preference.
  - Note that some of the victim groups included are historically more difficult to support or feel sympathy for (e.g., sexual offenders, correctional officers). This was done intentionally to expose students to the prevalence of victimization in various groups and to those victim groups' perspectives and challenges. In addition, several of the provided victim groups are large and diverse groups (e.g., adult offenders), and students can approach an advocacy initiative from a number of different angles. Students may need some guidance in the early stages of planning to help them identify a relevant target for their initiative and to think creatively about the issues faced by that victim group.
- Once groups have been created and victim groups randomly assigned or selected by each group, designate which type of advocacy initiative each group will create. Again, allow students to choose their preferred type of advocacy initiative or have them randomly select from some or all of the choices provided in Handout 6.3.
- There may be some victim groups and advocacy initiative types that are more challenging to combine than others. You may need to provide additional guidance to students who feel their randomly assigned combination is impossible or assign a different combination.
- Once victim group and advocacy initiative type have been determined for each group, go through Handout 6.1 with all students, explaining the activity parameters and the written summary expectations.
  - Explain to students that they will need to gather information and conduct some research on trends and challenges faced by their particular victim group. The materials and designs they prepare should be consistent with and reflect the information gathered in their research. This could also include interviewing members of the victim group or the potential members of the intended

audience for the advocacy initiative (e.g., elected officials; training participants; app users; witnesses of performance art, a protest, or a sit-in) to determine how best to engage those participants.

- Each group will prepare a presentation for the class about their advocacy initiative. This could include showing the video they prepared or describing the entire plan for a community event, for example. It will also include an explanation of possible outcome measures to ensure their initiative is effective.
- Each student or group must also prepare a brief written summary and reflection of the activity to be turned in at the beginning of the class group activity presentation day.

Activity Presentation Class Session

- On the day of group presentations, allow enough time for each group to present its advocacy initiative. Depending on the size of your class, this may require more than one class session.
- A possible presentation format could include the following:
  - Provide brief background information on the victim group, including prevalence of victimization, trends, and issues and challenges faced by this group before or as a result of their victimization.
  - Describe the advocacy initiative and how it will positively affect the victim group.
  - Describe potential outcome measures—how will they know their initiative was successful?
  - Time permitting, provide a brief reflection on students' participation in this activity, including how and why they decided on their particular approach, group members' ability to empathize with the victim group, and so on.

DEBRIEFING   At the end of the presentations, debrief the process of designing an advocacy initiative for various victimization groups.

Sample Discussion Questions

- Discuss the victim–perpetrator overlap.
- Which victim groups were easier to empathize with? Which were harder?
- Which types of advocacy initiatives seem like they would have the most impact, both short term and long term?

GRADING   Grading should be based on the content and quality of each student or group presentation. Appendix C: Presentation Grading Rubric can be used or modified for this activity. For group presentations, Appendix D: Group and Self-Evaluation Form can also be used or modified to assess each student's contribution to the overall presentation. If a written reflection paper or other written assignment is incorporated, Appendix A: Written Assignment Grading Rubric can be modified as appropriate.

MODIFICATIONS   *Varying Class Lengths*

- Depending on the size of the class, you may need multiple class sessions to accommodate all of the student presentations. Alternatively, have students videotape their presentations and post them in the online classroom platform (e.g., Blackboard), requiring everyone to view all the other groups' presentations.

■ This activity could also be assigned as a major project or final project to allow students the time to develop the proposal over the course of the semester and then actually carry out the initiative they designed (e.g., host a community event, create a blog, facilitate a public awareness campaign).

Varying Class Sizes

■ For smaller classes, each individual student could design his or her own advocacy initiative for a different victim group, or all students could focus on the same victim group but use different advocacy initiative formats.

■ For larger classes, an interesting variation would be to assign several groups the same victim group but with different advocacy initiatives. This would allow the class to see examples of various ways to advocate for the same population and narrow the overall class focus to one or just a few victim groups rather than every group being assigned a different victim group.

Online and/or Hybrid Courses

■ This can be an individual or group activity in an online course. For a group activity, it may be helpful to limit the types of advocacy initiatives from which students can choose (or you assign), given logistical complications and students' inability to work together in person.

■ If the online course has a synchronous component, consider requiring students to deliver their presentations, as described earlier, via video-conferencing technology. If the class is asynchronous, consider having students video record their presentations and post them for peer viewing. Alternatively, require students to submit a lengthy written description of the advocacy initiative using the format described in Handout 6.1.

RESOURCES

Bureau of Justice Statistics. (2015). *Data collection: National Crime Victimization Survey (NCVS)*. Retrieved from https://www.bjs.gov/index.cfm?ty=dcdetail&iid=245#Publications_and_products

Kennedy, S. (2016). Lights! Camera! Action projects! Engaging psychopharmacology students in service-based action projects focusing on student alcohol abuse. *Journal of Undergraduate Neuroscience Education, 14,* A138–A142.

National Institute of Justice. (2016). *Specific populations as victims*. Retrieved from https://nij.gov/topics/victims-victimization/Pages/specific-populations.aspx

7 TO PROTECT AND SERVE: TRAINING LAW ENFORCEMENT

Approximately 2 million jail bookings each year involve someone with a mental illness (Subramanian, Delaney, Roberts, Fishman, & McGarry, 2015). As a result, police officers and other first responders frequently come into contact with people with mental illness. It is increasingly more common for law enforcement officers to receive training specifically focused on mental health and mental illness and on the skills needed when interacting with this population. This activity gives students the chance to learn more about these types of training programs in general, including crisis intervention training (or CIT) programs, and the importance of implementing such trainings. In addition, students will consider how general information about mental illness can influence the work of law enforcement, as well as how such information is most effectively taught to law enforcement personnel. Students will design a brief training program targeted to law enforcement and deliver their training to the class.

LEARNING OBJECTIVES

Students will

(a) recognize the importance of providing training to law enforcement regarding psychology, mental health, crisis intervention, and other relevant topics;

(b) identify specific psychological concepts and how they can be useful to law enforcement (e.g., identifying signs of severe mental illness, how important body language can be, vulnerabilities of children with learning or emotional disorders, the effects of implicit bias on interacting with citizens of different racial groups);

(c) apply social science research skills and integrate empirical findings into training presentations;

(d) demonstrate group collaboration skills; and

(e) design a training program by engaging in a creative process, teaching a chosen topic to the class, and practicing oral communication skills.

PREPARATION

This activity is designed to take place over two class sessions. The first session will review the activity requirements and divide the class into small groups. During the second class session (likely a week or more later, as designated by the instructor), each small group will present its training to the class and, if possible, guest law enforcement officers.

---

http://dx.doi.org/10.1037/0000080-008

Activities for Teaching Psychology and Law: A Guide for Instructors, by A. D. Zelechoski, M. Wolbransky, and C. L. Riggs Romaine

Prior Didactic Coverage

This activity should take place after discussing the types of training law enforcement officers receive with regard to mental illness. Information from a textbook, training programs already implemented (such as CIT), or current events should be used to highlight the importance (and timeliness) of this topic (see Resources at the end of the activity for examples of several relevant articles). Students will use this background information as a basis for developing their own trainings for law enforcement and related personnel.

- History of the relationship between law enforcement and people with mental illness (including deinstitutionalization, criminalization, and related mental health policies)
- Importance of training law enforcement about mental illness (e.g., frequency of contact, stigma around increase in dangerousness)
- Current trainings developed to teach law enforcement about mental illness and the efficacy of these programs (e.g., CIT programs; see Content Note 7.1)
- Types of effective training methods and how to target training to officers. Have students consider how effective programs are delivered (e.g., interactive components, discussion, avoiding technical jargon) and effective methods of communication in general.

Materials Needed

- Handout 7.1: Training Law Enforcement Activity Worksheet (one copy for each student)
- Chalkboard or whiteboard (depending on the classroom) to list topics generated
- Equipment for small-group presentations (e.g., computer, projector, anything else groups require and request ahead of time)
- (Optional) Video showing a CIT or similar training (see Resources)
- (Optional) Predetermined small group assignments (three to six students per group)
- (Optional) Local law enforcement officers invited to sit in on training presentations and serve as guest judges or evaluators of each training. Officers can provide students with verbal or written feedback (or both). Handout 7.2: Law Enforcement Training Feedback Form is provided on the companion website.

Content Note 7.1. *Crisis Intervention Training (CIT) Programs*

- It is important to discuss the history and purpose of current training models developed to teach law enforcement about mental illness. This includes the "Memphis Model" CIT training (see Resources), which has been adopted by numerous jurisdictions nationwide.
- Part of a traditional CIT program is a 40-hour advanced officer training that has been shown to have various positive impacts on the officers and departments trained.
- It may be helpful to show students a short video of an actual CIT or similar training.
- Part of this didactic discussion should talk about why it is important to cover certain topics when training law enforcement (e.g., de-escalation, "suicide by cop"), how these topics might be chosen, and how this information is best communicated to law enforcement (i.e., why certain methods may be more effective than others when training law enforcement).

During the first class session, introduce the exercise, form small groups, and choose training topics. You may want to provide time for the groups to discuss what topic they would like to develop the training around or provide time for them to begin working on the actual training program design. During the second class session, each small group will present its training to the class. When planning the timing for this activity, consider the level of research and preparation you expect, and provide time between the first and second class periods accordingly. Students will likely need 1 to 2 weeks to develop their trainings.

Class 1

1. Activity Overview
   - Distribute Handout 7.1 to the class.
   - Explain the exercise and how it fits into the rest of the overall topic (e.g., police psychology, evaluating suspects, victimization).
   - Remind students about the increase in trainings for law enforcement officers related to psychology, communication, mental illness, and associated skills.
   - Explain that students work together in small groups for this activity and are asked to develop their own training for law enforcement officers, which they will then present to the class (and guest law enforcement officers, if possible).

2. Preparatory Discussion
   - Engage in a classroom discussion about what training topics students feel are the most important for law enforcement to receive. Topics should go beyond the scope of what has already been discussed in class and students should be encouraged to think about all of the topics throughout the semester when developing this list, as well as considering issues that arise in the media about police–community relations.
   - If time allows, continue this discussion as long as needed to allow the students to brainstorm as many ideas as they can. Be sure you have enough for the activity to be completed (i.e., one topic for each small group you plan to form).
   - Common topics you may want to include are as follows:
     - severe mental illness: identifying signs and communication strategies;
     - learning disabilities: communication and/or interrogation implications;
     - de-escalation strategies;
     - unconscious or implicit bias: how to identify, potential impacts;
     - age and suggestibility;
     - the use of body language when communicating with the public; and
     - trauma: how to identify and take into consideration during interactions/interviews.

3. Group Assignments
   - Divide the class into small groups (three to six students). Each group will be assigned a topic generated by the class.
   - You can assign topics by either (a) random assignment (e.g., pull topics out of a hat), or (b) have groups write down their top three topic choices and assign accordingly.

4. Presentation Guidelines
   - Each group will develop a training based on its assigned topic and present it to the rest of the class, as if the class were the targeted law enforcement students.
   - The "training" should be between 5 and 10 minutes long (which can be adjusted for each individual classroom) and can include a PowerPoint lecture, handouts, videos, group activity (e.g., demonstrations of different body positions and how it makes the other person feel, role-plays), and/or a short quiz at the end of the training to see whether the students learned the material.
     - *Optional evaluation component*: Consider requiring each group to create a short evaluation for their training to see whether their training was effective (such questions or assessments are common in real-world professional trainings). These should include questions about the key concepts covered in the training. These questions could be given to the class after the training day and/or included in a class exam. This provides students with an opportunity to develop research skills and evaluate the effectiveness of their project, and will provide you with feedback about class participation and project efficacy overall.
   - Allow small groups to work on this during class to provide an opportunity to talk with each group individually. Then give them time outside of class to research and put together the training (at least 1 week, if not longer, is recommended). Following are tips for helping students prepare their presentations:
     - Think about the video watched in class or trainings that were discussed (if applicable). What was most effective or ineffective about those trainings?
     - Who is the audience? (Law enforcement officers)
     - With what characteristics may they be coming to training, and how do you use these to your advantage?
     - How can you maintain attention and interest during trainings?
     - The goal is to provide assistance based on the topic, not to tell officers what they should or should not do for their job. Discuss why this is important (e.g., trainers are often not officers themselves; police have other things to consider during real-life situations).
   - Assign a day dedicated to the in-class trainings.

Class 2

1. Have each group present its training to the class and guest law enforcement officers, if applicable.
   - *Inviting actual officers:* Consider inviting campus or local police officers to attend one or both of these class sessions. For example, the chief of public safety could attend the first class to discuss the need for such trainings or could attend the second class to "participate" in each group's training and provide feedback to the class accordingly. This provides students with a law enforcement perspective and facilitates important dialogue between students and public or campus safety personnel.
2. Allow time for students to complete evaluations either after each training or at the end of the class (after all presentations are finished).

DEBRIEFING After all of the groups present their trainings, have a class discussion about the activity. This will help students debrief about the challenges in developing such trainings, their perspectives of law enforcement, and how the project impacted their overall views.

Sample Discussion Questions

- What did you learn about the importance of these training programs?
- What were the challenges your group faced when creating your training program?
- How did it feel to put yourself in the shoes of a trainer for law enforcement? Of a "police officer student"?
- Did this project affect your view of law enforcement? Why or why not? If so, how?
- Were any of your personal views otherwise affected by this exercise?
- How do we ensure that these training programs are effective?
- As the "trainees" (i.e., law enforcement officers), how did you react to the material?
- What methods were most effective?

GRADING Grading for this activity can be based on the group project or each individual's performance, or both. You can choose how to divide the final grade breakdown between the two (e.g., make group and individual grades each 50% of the final grade, or one worth more than the other). It is most important that the grading scheme reflects your goals for this activity and that it is clearly communicated to students during the first class session. Appendix C: Presentation Grading Rubric can be used and/or modified for this activity.

For example, each student's grade could be calculated based on the following:

1. Group work: training content, including clear use of social science research to inform the presentation of the chosen topic; training method, including
   - evidence the group took the audience into consideration (i.e., law enforcement officers),
   - creativity of the presentation/training, and
   - effectiveness of the training delivery format.
2. Individual work: Completion of a written evaluation form (see, e.g., Appendix D: Group and Self-Evaluation Form), which could include content-based questions or subjective experience related to the project overall. Group member participation, which could include the following:
   - observations of individual student during the group oral presentation;
   - an individual component, such as a journal entry, reflection paper, or short essay about the project and the student's experience;
   - observations of individual student as the law enforcement students during the training day (e.g., were engaged, respectful); and
   - use of Appendix C: Presentation Grading Rubric.

ACTIVITY MODIFICATIONS *Varying Class Lengths*

- It is important to adequately cover the background didactic information described earlier in the activity as well as to provide students with an opportunity to discuss effective methods of providing such training to law enforcement specifically. If class time is limited, topics can be assigned to groups and groups assigned to work together outside of class.

- You can set up individual meetings with small groups between the time topics are chosen and projects are presented as an alternative to using in-class time.
- Trainings can also be shortened (or lengthened) depending on class time allocated to this activity.
- Providing time after the projects are presented is important to allow students to debrief as needed. An alternative is to hand out evaluation forms (or create an electronic version) on which students can provide feedback, thoughts, and reactions to the activity. This is valuable for both you and the students.

Varying Class Sizes

- Group size can and should be adjusted according to class size, but small groups should be kept to three to six students to allow all students to participate in the presentation of the training (Beebe & Masterson, 2003; Booth, 1996).

Online and/or Hybrid Courses

- This activity can be completed in both online and hybrid classes.
- If possible, introduce the activity in the traditional classroom (i.e., for hybrid classes). This will allow students the chance to ask questions and for you to clarify any confusion as needed.
- If instructions are provided solely online, you should create a place where questions can be asked and answered so that all students can view and benefit accordingly. If one student has the question, it is likely that others have the same question.
- Be sure to give students sufficient time to work together in their small groups. Students in online classes may need more time allotted than in traditional classroom settings—at least initially—to set up their plan for how they will work together. It is important for online instructors to check in on small groups shortly after posting the group assignments.
- Instructors of hybrid classes may choose to have groups present their trainings as outlined earlier. If this is not possible, groups can video or audio record their trainings and upload them to a group discussion board where the rest of the class can view the trainings.
- Every student may then be asked to post follow-up questions to the "instructors" (i.e., small group members), feedback, and/or reactions to the trainings themselves. It is also possible to assign this project as individual work instead of group work. Grading schemes would need to be modified accordingly.

RESOURCES   Use YouTube to search for current videos depicting CIT trainings.

Compton, M. T., Bahora, M., Watson, A. C., & Oliva, J. R. (2008). A comprehensive review of extant research on crisis intervention team (CIT) programs. *Journal of the American Academy of Psychiatry and the Law Online, 36,* 47–55.

Compton, M. T., Bakeman, R., Broussard, B., Hankerson-Dyson, D., Husbands, L., Krishan, S., . . . & Watson, A. C. (2014). The police-based crisis intervention team (CIT) model: II. Effects on level of force and resolution, referral, and arrest. *Psychiatric Services, 65*, 523–529.

Goode, E. (2016, April 25). For police, a playbook for conflicts involving mental illness. *New York Times*. Retrieved from http://www.nytimes.com/2016/04/26/health/police-mental-illness-crisis-intervention.html

Steadman, H. J., & Morrissette, D. (2016). Police responses to persons with mental illness: Going beyond CIT Training. *Psychiatric Services, 67*, 1054–1056.

University of Memphis CIT Center. (n.d.). *National Alliance on Mental Illness CIT training manual and national curriculum*. Retrieved from http://cit.memphis.edu/curriculuma.php?id=0

REFERENCES

Beebe, S. A., & Masterson, J. T. (2003). *Communicating in small groups*. Boston, MA: Pearson Education.

Booth, A. (1996). Assessing group work. In A. Booth & P. Hyland (Eds.), *History in higher education* (pp. 276–297). Oxford, England: Blackwell.

Subramanian, R., Delaney, R., Roberts, S., Fishman, N., & McGarry, P. (2015). *Incarceration's front door: The misuse of jails in America*. Vera Institute of Justice. Retrieved from http://www.vera.org/sites/default/files/resources/downloads/incarcerations-front-door report.pdf

8 DO YOU SEE WHAT I SEE? EYEWITNESS IDENTIFICATION

The purpose of this activity is to introduce and demonstrate the malleable nature of memory and challenges to eyewitness recollection, especially for events that may not have seemed important at the time they occurred. Using a confederate, the "incident" will occur in the classroom and students will be asked to recall detailed information. Students will have the experience of being an eyewitness and be able to compare the challenges they faced to the empirical findings on eyewitness accuracy and subsequent course coverage of the topic.

LEARNING OBJECTIVES

Students will

(a) learn about the malleable nature of memory and the factors that may influence how events are recalled,
(b) experience factors that may influence eyewitness accuracy,
(c) demonstrate an understanding of how intervening misinformation affected recollection of events, and
(d) describe the impact of various photo-array procedures on identification (optional).

PREPARATION

Prior Didactic Coverage

- Because this activity is intended to be an introduction to the challenges and limits of eyewitness testimony, no background information is required for students.
- For instructors, readings are suggested in the Resources section for further information in preparing for various discussion components throughout the activity.

Materials Needed

- A willing confederate (see further instructions in the Facilitation section).
- A predetermined scenario and props as needed (e.g., a forgotten book, jacket).
- If including the optional photo lineup (described subsequently), collect photographs and create slides presenting the photo arrays.

http://dx.doi.org/10.1037/0000080-009
Activities for Teaching Psychology and Law: A Guide for Instructors, by A. D. Zelechoski, M. Wolbransky, and C. L. Riggs Romaine

Before the Activity

- *Recruiting a confederate and planning for the "incident":* Recruit a willing confederate to help with this activity.
  - The confederate can be a fellow instructor, student, or staff member. Ideally, this person should not be someone known to the class. A student from the class or another psychology professor from your small department will not work as easily if most of the students can readily identify the person. If the class meets in a building with administrative assistants, graduate students, or other staff, they may be able to visit your classroom for the one to three minutes required for this activity, assuming they would not be familiar to most of your students.
  - Give the available space and resources, design a plausible reason for the confederate to enter the room and then leave, with minimal interaction with you or the students.
    - A "forgotten" item provides one easy option. For example, the confederate can enter the classroom and walk up and across the front of the room to retrieve the forgotten jacket, folder, or USB drive from the classroom computer.
    - This requires minimal, if any, interaction from you, and class can proceed as usual as the confederate enters and leaves in the background.
  - Plan and establish timing and details of the interaction with the confederate ahead of time. To do so, you will need to have detailed information about what actually occurred, which will allow for comparison to what students recall and how the story may be conflated over the course of discussion. Be sure to plan for and take note of the following:
    - the confederate's physical description, including (a) gender and race/ethnicity (see Content Note 8.1); (b) approximate height; (c) approximate weight; (d) hair color, length, and style; and (e) clothing style and color;
    - the time the confederate entered the classroom and amount of time spent in the classroom;
    - if there are multiple exits, where the confederate entered and left the classroom; and
    - the observed reason for entering the classroom (e.g., what item was retrieved and from where).
- *Details within the "incident":* The level of detail and planning for this activity can vary, depending on whether it is used as an introductory demonstration

---

Content Note 8.1. *The Other Race Effect*

Research indicates individuals have more difficulty identifying individuals of another race than they do identifying, and distinguishing, members of their own race (Meisner & Brigham, 2001). This is a general finding that is often cited in instances of cross-race identification (i.e., when the eyewitness and alleged perpetrator are different races) and could be discussed during the activity, if relevant, or later if this topic is covered in class.

---

or focus for discussion. Some key details may provide more opportunities for discussion.

- ○ The confederate can be asked to wear a hat or shirt with writing of some sort, to provide another detail students (i.e., the eyewitnesses) may recall. Immediately recognizable logos (e.g., for your school or the local professional sports team) may be too easily identified, but words or a logo for a lesser known company provide another detail for recall and discussion and may demonstrate possible errors in memory. Students may also be asked to describe the pattern or colors of clothing.
- ○ The specific action and movements of the confederate can also be used as relevant details. Consider establishing with the confederate exactly what he or she will do (e.g., place the USB drive in the right front pants pocket before walking out of the classroom). This will allow for more specific questions about what occurred.

Part 1: The "Incident"

- ■ Begin or continue class as usual. Ideally, you should be speaking to the class, with students' general attention on you and/or visual aids near you.
- ■ As the "incident" occurs (e.g., the confederate enters the room, retrieves an item, and leaves), continue with class as usual with minimal interruption or acknowledgment of the confederate.

Part 2: Recalling What Was Observed

- ■ Several minutes later, walk to the area of the classroom where the confederate engaged in the orchestrated activity (e.g., from where the confederate retrieved the "forgotten" item) and appear concerned. Ask the class, "Did you see the person who came in here? I think (s)he took my ____."
  - ○ *To accuse or not to accuse?* Accusing the confederate of taking something (on purpose or by mistake) adds an element of importance and intensity often present in eyewitness scenarios. You could state that a phone, keys, or USB drive were picked up by the confederate. This does add deception to the activity, and you will need to carefully debrief students after the activity concludes and be clear that the confederate was assisting you with the activity and did nothing wrong or questionable. Treating the incident as a mistake may balance the pros and cons, raising the importance without assigning malice to the individual. Note that a well-intentioned student may attempt to go look for the confederate or otherwise intervene to retrieve your item, and you may need to stop him or her.
  - ○ If you prefer to avoid accusation, the activity can still work. Simply stop the class and ask students to try to recall the individual who came in and out several minutes ago. Proceed with the outlined discussion without the cover story of why. Students may be more aware this was a class demonstration, but the effects of memory and attention will still be demonstrated.

- Lead the students in volunteering as many details as they can recall about what occurred. Take careful note of what students report, watching for statements that may be slightly or entirely inaccurate and could get incorporated into students' memory of the event. Also note whether any students state that they do not know, or if they attempt to remember or suggest something of use. Be sure to ask students about the following:
  - What time did the person come in?
  - What was he or she wearing?
    - Clothing style?
    - Colors?
    - Unique features (writing or logos on clothing)?
  - How tall was the person? And how big (approximate body weight)?
  - Age? Gender? Race/ethnicity?
  - Where did the person come in and out?
  - Did you see where he or she headed?
- If no inaccurate details are stated in discussion, try to plant one. Add a detail that is false, but not contradictory, to anything that occurred (e.g., stating the individual had a nose ring or visible tattoo on the arm) or add information that contradicts what was observed (e.g., stating the confederate wore green sneakers, when really the sneakers were red). Note if this detail is repeated, contradicted, or otherwise comes up in students' reports.
  - *Getting a description*: You may choose how "in character" to be for this portion. To simulate a real situation as closely as possible, you can appear concerned and state that you were focused on the class topic and did not see what happened. You can then ask for help in getting a description of who came in and what occurred so that you can describe the situation to an administrative assistant or security personnel to help retrieve the lost item. Alternatively, you may simply ask for a description and test the limits of the students' recollection.
- After discussion, ask students to take a piece of paper and write down what they recall from the incident in as much detail as possible. You may collect these observations to look for themes, or ask students to keep them and refer to them in the following discussion.
- An additional optional component to incorporate is a photo lineup.
  - *Optional photo lineup*: To add the experience of identifying a suspect from a photo array, you can create a "lineup" of photographs. One easy way to do this is using projected slides (e.g., PowerPoint) that can be viewed by the whole class at once. In advance, take five to eight photographs of individuals who would match a description of the confederate and a photograph of the confederate. These photographs should be headshots that show faces with minimal background. Two variations can be used, independently or together, to illustrate and explore important concepts from the literature:
    - Research indicates that witnesses are more accurate in their identification when presented with photos sequentially (thereby comparing each photograph to the memory of the individual) rather than simultaneously (when faces might be compared with one another). To test this finding in class, create two photo arrays. The first should show all photographs at once (on the same slide). Label photos as A, B, C, and so on. The second photo array should be a series

of slides, with one photograph per slide, also labeled A, B, C, and so on. Have half of the class view one array, and record which photo was the person they saw come into the classroom. Have the other half view the second array and record the same information. (If using slides to show the photographs, ask students in the other group to close their eyes or turn around so as not to see the other array.)

- The research also indicates that people are more likely to misidentify an innocent person when the actual perpetrator is *not* in the array and the witness has not been notified of this possibility. To illustrate and test this finding, do not include the confederate in either photo array. Ask students to identify which photograph shows the person they saw in the classroom.

  ○ If the photo lineup is included in the activity, incorporate the preceding issues in the discussion in Part 3. Survey how many students picked each photograph, and have them compare the experience of evaluating the sequential versus simultaneous lineup. Compare the results of the two types of photo lineup administration.

Part 3: Discussion of What Occurred

To begin discussion, note for students that they were just eyewitnesses to an event and engaged in a process similar to what an eyewitness in the legal system might do when reporting events to the police.

Ask students to report their written recollections of the incident.

- Note and discuss any inaccurate details that were incorporated into reports. (Also see Content Notes 8.1 and 8.2.)
- If you planted any inaccurate information, note this for students and evaluate whether and how it was incorporated into their recall of the incident's details.
- Observe and discuss the level of details students recalled.
- Compare their estimates of height and weight to your information about the confederate. How easy or hard is it to estimate these from observations?
- How accurate were descriptions of clothing and hair?
- What details were recalled, and what details were not? Was this consistent across students, or was there variation?
- Did students explicitly state what they did *not* recall? Was there any perceived pressure to come up with or fill in details?
- If relevant (given the racial and ethnic background of both the confederate and the students), how might the race/ethnicity of the individual influence eyewitness memory and recall?

Content Note 8.2.   *The Misinformation Effect*

Postevent information has been consistently shown to influence individual's memory of the event and may be incorporated into memories of the event (for a review of eyewitness memory generally, see Brainerd & Reyna, 2005; Loftus, 2005; or Wells & Loftus, 2013).

- Lead the class in a discussion of the experience of being a witness. Important topics to highlight include the following:
  - the challenge of recalling details of an event that did not appear important when it occurred—note this may be the case for many witnesses who were indirectly involved or circumstantial witnesses to an event (as opposed to the victim);
  - whether and to what extent inaccurate details were included or influential to recollections;
  - how this may have been different had the confederate engaged in some extreme or threatening behavior or displayed a weapon at the time of the event (see Content Note 8.3); and
  - if a photo lineup was used, discuss its use and its impact on students' ability to identify the individual.
- Discuss the potential ramifications of any misidentifications that were made. Have students consider how this would affect an investigation (potentially focusing the authorities on the wrong individual), the person identified (an innocent person now in the position of defending himself or herself from accusation), and the victim (delays in justice and resolution of the issues).
- Debrief any deception that occurred during the activity. Be sure to note explicitly that the individual was a confederate you recruited and that no crime, errors, or wrongdoing occurred.

DEBRIEFING   Although previous discussions embedded into the activity will have allowed for debriefing of many aspects of the activity, it may still be helpful to formally debrief the overall experience.

Sample Discussion Questions

- What additional or overall observations do you have about the activity or the experience of participating?
- What did you find most challenging?
- What pressures did you feel? How did you feel if you did not know the requested information? That is, did you feel pressure to recall or come up with an answer?
- *Note.* If students were inaccurate in their reports or fell prey to common errors in memory, it will be important to normalize this experience and note how errors in memory are typically the rule and not the exception.

This activity can serve as a helpful reference and example as the class continues to learn about eyewitnesses, eyewitness testimony, and issues around misidentification and wrongful convictions. In subsequent lectures and class discussions, you can ask students to reflect and apply their experience from the activity by considering how a discussed phenomenon (e.g., certainty of the eyewitness, cross-race identification, simultaneous vs.

Content Note 8.3. *The Weapon Effect*

A large body of research has examined the impact of *weapon focus effect*, the tendency of a witness to focus attention on a weapon and therefore have a less accurate or less detailed recollection of the perpetrator or event (see Steblay, 1992).

sequential photo presentation) did or did not occur in the activity or may have influenced memory for this event.

GRADING

This activity would most likely be assessed generally as part of participation in the course, as it is an entirely in-class group experience with little material produced. To record and give students credit for participation, their written observations (and identification from the photo lineup, if used) could be collected. These should not be graded for quality or extent of memory (which could vary in relation to a number of factors unrelated to the student's effort and engagement) but could be awarded participation points for completion. Collecting students' recollections also allows you to compile and analyze the accuracies and inaccuracies in their reports to use as illustrations when different aspects of eyewitness identification and testimony are discussed. Appendix B: Participation Grading Rubric can be used or modified for this activity.

MODIFICATIONS

Varying Class Lengths

- If less time is available, you may choose to spend less time in discussion and instead have students write their reflections.
- The activity can also be used at the end of one class period to introduce the topic for the following class meeting.
  - In between, students can complete reading on the topic and discuss their experience in light of their readings in the following class.
  - If the activity is divided between class periods, be sure to debrief any deception that occurred before students leave the classroom. It would be unethical to leave students with the impression that a crime, at worst, or even a questionable misunderstanding had occurred when a simulation had taken place.

Varying Class Sizes

- In large classes, it may be particularly important to have the students write their recollections, thereby actively engaging all students in the process of recalling the event, rather than just a few of the more outspoken students.

Online and/or Hybrid Courses

- The challenge for this activity is making the "incident" available for all to see.
- Given the ease of filming provided by current technology, you can enlist a confederate and video record the incident using a cell phone or digital video camera and then upload the video to the course site. This could be done as a brief video to watch, or could involve the same aspects as the class demonstration and occur in the background as you talk about another class topic (with the premise that you were filmed at a live lecture).
- Alternatively, you may take advantage of the numerous videos available online for demonstrations of eyewitness limitations. Videos are available depicting crowded outdoor scenes or other events and may include follow-up questions about what occurred in the scene.

- You may also choose to use a movie or news clip available online. Find one that includes an otherwise inconspicuous event that occurs in the background of the main action. The following instructions and related prompts could be modified for any video.
- Instruct students to watch the video once and then respond to the prompts for individual written responses.
  - Ask students to write down their recollection of what occurred in as much detail as possible.
  - Students can also be asked to respond to specific questions such as the following:
    - What was the individual wearing?
      - Clothing style?
      - Colors?
      - Unique features?
    - How tall was the person? What was his or her approximate weight?
    - Age? Gender? Race/ethnicity?
    - From which direction did the person come? Where was he or she headed?
- After students learn more about the topic (from class materials, lectures, or reading), ask them to write one or two pages of reflection on how the various concepts related to eyewitness identification could be observed in their recollection of the event or could have influenced how they recalled details about the event.

RESOURCES

For additional information, summary chapters written for professionals and trainees may be particularly helpful (e.g., Wells & Loftus, 2013).

Amicus curiae briefs written by the American Psychological Association on the topic of eyewitness identification research (available online at http://www.apa.org/about/offices/ogc/amicus/index-issues.aspx) also provide helpful summaries of the eyewitness research. If assigned, these briefs may also serve as an introduction to how amicus briefs are structured and organized in preparation for Activity 16: May It Please the Court: Amicus Curiae Brief.

REFERENCES

Brainerd, C. J., & Reyna, V. F. (2005). *The science of false memory*. Oxford, England: Oxford University Press. http://dx.doi.org/10.1093/acprof:oso/9780195154054.001.0001

Loftus, E. F. (2005). Planting misinformation in the human mind: A 30-year investigation of the malleability of memory. *Learning & Memory, 12*, 361–366. http://dx.doi.org/10.1101/lm.94705

Meisner, C., & Brigham, J. C. (2001). Twenty years of investigating the own-race bias in memory for faces: A meta-analytic review. *Psychology, Public Policy, and Law, 7*, 3–35. http://dx.doi.org/10.1037/1076-8971.7.1.3

Steblay, N. M. (1992). A meta-analytic review of the weapon focus effect. *Law and Human Behavior, 16*, 413–424. http://dx.doi.org/10.1007/BF02352267

Wells, G. L., & Loftus, E. F. (2013). Eyewitness memory for people and events. In R. K. Otto & I. B. Weiner (Eds.), *Handbook of psychology* (2nd ed., Vol. 11, pp. 617–629). Hoboken, NJ: Wiley.

9

TO WAIVE OR NOT TO WAIVE?
Miranda RIGHTS AND DUE PROCESS

The purpose of this activity is to demonstrate the complicated "totality of circumstances" that are considered in the evaluation of a suspect's waiver of Miranda rights and the subsequent determination of whether a person's statements can be used against him or her as evidence. Using hypothetical case scenarios, students will apply what they have learned about (a) due process protections, (b) Miranda v. Arizona (1966) and subsequent court decisions, (c) the psycholegal research on factors that influence comprehension of the Miranda warning, and (d) the process of forensic mental health assessment of Miranda waivers.

LEARNING OBJECTIVES

Students will

    (a) demonstrate an understanding of factors that the courts have recognized as influencing the admissibility of statements made during police interrogations;

    (b) apply factual knowledge of due process protections from readings and class discussion to case material;

    (c) develop an understanding of how previous court decisions can be applied to facts in a hypothetical case;

    (d) learn about the psychological and psycholegal issues forensic evaluators assess while conducting this type of evaluation; and

    (e) continue to develop oral argument and teamwork skills, presenting conclusions and rationales to the class.

PREPARATION

Prior Didactic Coverage

- *Miranda* warning and relevant court decisions (see Content Note 9.1)
  - This activity requires students to have some familiarity with the basis and history of the *Miranda* warning (including the right against self-incrimination) and the cases that followed and defined the *Miranda v. Arizona* (1966) decision.
  - Because most students will be familiar with the *Miranda* warning itself, be sure to explain the connection between giving and waiving these rights and the court's subsequent determination regarding the admissibility of statements made during police interrogations.
- Basic principles of forensic mental health assessment
- Specific criteria examined in an evaluation of an individual's capacity to waive *Miranda* rights (see Content Note 9.2)
- Research on factors associated with *Miranda*-related deficits (see Content Note 9.3)

http://dx.doi.org/10.1037/0000080-010
Activities for Teaching Psychology and Law: A Guide for Instructors, by A. D. Zelechoski, M. Wolbransky, and C. L. Riggs Romaine

Content Note 9.1. *Relevant Court Rulings*

The following cases and topics are applicable and will be helpful during the current activity. You may choose to talk about cases that establish precedent by name or simply discuss their holdings, depending on the course level and time available.

- *Brown v. Mississippi* (1936)—held that physical coercion (violence) violates the 14th Amendment
- *Spano v. New York* (1959)—established the concept of an individual's "free will over-borne" and prohibition against psychological coercion
- *Colorado v. Connelly* (1986)—clarified that these protections are specifically against coercion from police; coercion from other forces such as mental illness do not affect admissibility (at least not in this context)
- *Escobedo v. Illinois* (1964)—found that suspects have a constitutional right to counsel during interrogations
- *Berghuis v. Thompkins* (2010)—held that a waiver of rights cannot be passive, via silence, but must be invoked verbally
- *Salinas v. Texas* (2013)—found that a defendant's silence in the face of specific questions during noncustodial police interrogation can be used against him or her
- *Coyote v. United States* (1967)—established the totality of circumstances test to evaluate *Miranda* waiver; includes age, intelligence, prior contact with the police, conduct, physical conditions, background, education, intellectual functioning, literacy, and mental illness
- *J.D.B. v. North Carolina* (2011)—established the reasonable person test to determine whether interrogation is "custodial"

State courts have varied in their rulings on the permissibility of promises of leniency (e.g., vague statements that "things will go better" or promises of a less serious charge) and misrepresentation of evidence (e.g., telling the suspect her fingerprints were found at the scene). Generally, these practices have not been barred per se but are considered within the totality of circumstances (for a summary, see Goldstein, Goldstein, Zelle, & Condie, 2013).

Content Note 9.2. *Mental Health Evaluation of a* Miranda *Waiver*

In this activity, students are asked to identify the key issues a forensic mental health evaluator would need to assess in the hypothetical case provided. To do this, the following topics should be reviewed:

1. The *forensic evaluation process*. Specifically, you should review the fact that forensic evaluations are conducted to address a specific legal question, as well as the general process of gathering collateral information, records, and interviewing the defendant. Most psychology and law textbooks will provide an introduction to this process and may provide information on *Miranda* waiver evaluations specifically.
2. The concept of *functional abilities*—that is, what a person must be able to do or understand to competently waive *Miranda* rights (e.g., understand the terminology used and the meaning of a right). Summary book chapters and review articles may also be helpful to provide this information (e.g., Goldstein et al., 2013).

Content Note 9.3. *Factors Associated With Deficits in* Miranda *Comprehension*

An extensive body of research has examined aspects of the *Miranda* warning (e.g., reading level, verbal vs. written presentation) and the individual (e.g., intellectual functioning, age) that may be associated with deficits in *Miranda* comprehension (for a review of this research, see Goldstein et al., 2013).

Materials Needed

- Handout 9.1: Case Summaries with Instructor Notes (one copy)
- Handout 9.2: The Questioning of James (copies for one third of groups)
- Handout 9.3: The Questioning of Hannah (copies for one third of groups)
- Handout 9.4: The Questioning of Sarah (copies for one third of groups)

FACILITATION

Part 1: Review and Discuss Cases in Small Groups

- Divide the class into small groups (i.e., three to six students), and give each group one of the three cases. For larger classes, multiple groups may use the same case.
- Instruct the class to carefully review the assigned scenarios before working together to identify all aspects of the scenario (e.g., the suspect's age, intellectual functioning, length of interrogation) that are legally relevant and should be considered when determining whether each suspect's statements would be admissible in court.
  1. For each aspect, the group should make a "ruling" as to whether, in this given case, this aspect would make the statements admissible or inadmissible. Students should be prepared to share their rationale.
  2. Of the multiple relevant aspects in the scenarios, each group should determine the issue that is key (i.e., the factor that is most influential in the current case and should be the basis for a decision on admissibility), and prepare to explain their reasoning and their "ruling" about admissibility for the whole case, based on this key factor.
  3. Assuming this suspect's waiver of *Miranda* rights is under question in court, what key questions would a forensic evaluator need to assess in evaluating the suspect's capacity? What specific functional abilities would the evaluator examine?
- As the groups work, circulate among them and assist students in identifying and considering the key aspects (Handout 9.1 includes all three case scenarios and instructor notes regarding the key aspects of each case). It may be helpful to suggest students refer to their assigned readings and notes to help identify relevant precedents and issues.
  o *Identifying key evaluation topics:* Students may need help identifying relevant case aspects that might raise concerns for a defense attorney or mental health evaluator. It may be helpful to ask questions such as the following: "Do any aspects of this case or the defendant sound familiar from the *Miranda* literature? Are there things a lawyer would be concerned about?" or "Does this defendant have any traits or characteristics that have been associated with *Miranda* deficits in the literature?"
  o *Forming arguments and "it depends":* The court has largely declined to establish specific factors that make a *Miranda* waiver inadmissible per se, relying instead on the *totality of circumstances* test to evaluate the myriad factors present in a given case. As such, most details included in each case would not make the suspect's waiver automatically invalid but would be one of many factors considered and argued as relevant in the case. Notes provided to the instructor in Handout 9.1 raise questions to consider (and for students

to argue for or against). Students may need help identifying arguments for or against admissibility. Help groups identify both sides of the issues and form arguments to defend why a factor should or should not be considered in the current case.

■ Provide approximately 15 minutes for discussion and analysis in small groups (or more time, if feasible).

The Cases

The Questioning of James. James Parsons, age 32, is a resident in a local group home for people with severe and persistent mental health disorders. He has been diagnosed with schizophrenia and has a history of auditory hallucinations and paranoid thinking. As a young man, he received special education services and was diagnosed with mild intellectual disability. There have been a series of eight incidents in the neighborhood around the group home involving general destruction of property. James was identified as matching the description provided by witnesses. Several months ago, he was picked up at 10:00 a.m. by local police, taken to the police station, and read his *Miranda* rights. He signed the waiver of his rights and spoke briefly with police about general information, including the location of his group home. At 4:00 p.m., James had not made any incriminating statements. He was not offered any breaks from the small interrogation room, nor was he offered any food. By 6:00 p.m., James began to pace around the interrogation room, speaking inaudibly to himself. By 9:00 p.m., James sat, resting his head on the table and occasionally responding to what appeared to be auditory hallucinations, stating, "No, I don't want to," "I can't, I didn't." According to police records, at 10:00 p.m., James gave a verbal and written confession, stating that he had committed each of the eight incidents.

The Questioning of Hannah. There have been a series of thefts at High Valley Middle School, including high-value laptop computers, tablets, and cell phones. The police were called to the school. The school principal retrieves Hannah, age 12, from her math class and escorts her to a conference room, where two police offers and the vice principal are seated. Hannah is asked to have a seat as the vice principal closes the door and takes a seat at the table. The police officers ask Hannah questions about what she has seen and heard and remind her that "honesty is the best policy," while implying that they have concerns that she may have been involved. If Hannah makes statements that are incriminating, would they be admissible in court?

The Questioning of Sarah. Sarah is a 43-year-old woman who lives with her two children on the north side of town. Recently, a young man was hit by a car on her street. He remains in critical condition, unable to provide any information about the event. The police have questioned all of the residents on the block. When the police questioned Sarah at the station, she declined to answer questions and said she did not wish to talk to them without an attorney present. Two weeks later, the police again ask Sarah to come to the station to answer questions. They offer her a ride to the station in a squad car and read her the *Miranda* warning before they began questioning her. After 5 hours with no breaks, Sarah has not made any statements and has remained quiet as the officers talk and tell her what they suspect occurred. Sarah is offered only water, and the police continue to question her late into the night, for an additional 4 hours. Although the police have yet to find any evidence in the case, they tell Sarah that traces of the victim's blood were found on her car. They also tell her that if she tells the truth, the district attorney will charge her with a less severe offense and she can likely avoid jail time. According to police records, Sarah then confessed to her involvement in the accident, 10 hours after she was originally brought to the station. Are Sarah's statements admissible in court?

Part 2: Presentation and Class Discussion of Cases

- Have the class come back together for a large-group discussion.
- Begin by reading, or asking a student to read, one case scenario. This will be the first time other groups hear the case material for that scenario.
- Ask the group to report to the class:
  - What aspects of the scenario may be legally relevant when determining admissibility? What is your "ruling" and rationale for each aspect?
  - What issue did you determine was key in this scenario?
  - If this defendant's waiver was under question in court, what key aspects would an evaluator need to examine? In what functional abilities is the evaluator interested?
- To illustrate the adversarial and "it depends" nature of these determinations, ask someone from another group to frame an opposing argument (e.g., if the group argues a youth was not free to leave a classroom conversation with police, an opposing argument would be that students leave classrooms on a regular basis, could suggest investigating whether this youth has a history of walking out of class, and note that a reasonable person of this youth's age would not feel it was a custodial setting).
- Repeat this series of questions for each of the three cases.
  - *Time management and depth of discussion:* This discussion can be modified to take more time or less time, depending on class timing. Answering the provided questions for each case and having some discussion requires at least 5 minutes per case. Discussion can easily be extended and given both depth and further application by asking the following:
    - Follow-up questions about rulings: Ask students which cases established precedents and factors they refer to (e.g., it was *J.D.B. v. North Carolina* (2011) that established the "reasonable person" test to determine whether Hannah would believe she was in custody).
    - Follow-up questions to develop counterarguments: How could an attorney argue in opposition to your conclusion?
    - Follow-up questions to delve into evaluation: How would an evaluator assess the defendant's understanding? Would any of the forensic assessment tools the students have read or discussed be relevant in this case? What kind of collateral sources would be helpful to the evaluator?
- Wrap up by briefly discussing the common themes across cases and those uniquely important within certain cases.

Lead the class in a brief discussion of what it was like to apply case law and general (nomothetic) information to a specific individual in this case scenario (ideographic).

Sample Discussion Questions

- What was it like to try to apply the case law?
- Did certain aspects immediately stand out to you as legally relevant?
- Are there areas where more definition and clarity about what is allowed would be helpful from the courts?
- What was it like to weigh the totality of circumstance in the case? How did you decide which factors to weigh more heavily?
- Are there specific concerns you would have in any of these cases?
- Are there factors that seem important but may not be legally relevant?

GRADING   This activity may be assessed as part of "participation" in the course, or can be assigned value as a course assignment. For participation credit, grading should be based on each student's engagement in the activity and his or her use of the available information. Appendix B: Participation Grading Rubric can be used or modified for this purpose. Clarity and strength of arguments, as well as application of relevant case law and research findings, can be considered for inclusion as participation grading elements.

Alternatively, or in addition, a written assignment can be incorporated. For example, given the large body of research on the *Miranda* warning and comprehension of *Miranda* rights, you may use this topic as an opportunity to have students read original research.

- Depending on the course level, assign students to search the literature and summarize relevant findings or bring a particularly interesting or helpful article to class.
- Original research papers may also be assigned as reading assignments. Use or modify Appendix A: Written Assignment Grading Rubric, as appropriate.

MODIFICATIONS *Varying Class Lengths*

- This activity can easily fill an 80-minute class session, depending on the depth of discussion and the number of groups reporting back to the class.
- For shorter class sessions or other time constraints, you may assign cases in one class session and discuss in the following session.
  - Small-group preparation and discussion could take place between sessions as homework or be assigned as individual homework before small group discussion in the next session. This would shorten the time needed for the small groups to confer.

Varying Class Sizes

- For larger classes, this activity can be facilitated in a number of ways, such as having multiple small groups use the same case.

- Small seminar-style classes may have just one group per case but, in many cases, multiple groups will have discussed the same case. There are different ways to approach discussion of the cases:
  - Have each group that discussed the case answer the question before moving on to the next question. Compare and contrast what different groups saw as "key" and how they argued or explained their rationales.
  - Have small groups come together for a few minutes before the whole class discussion. Allow them 5 minutes to compare findings and determine what they think are the most important aspects and most convincing arguments to support them.
  - Have small groups submit their responses on paper before the class as a whole engages in a discussion of the key factors influencing each case. You may use students' responses to call on certain groups to provide specific points, including differences between the groups.
- Regardless of total class size, it may be helpful to maintain a true small group format (i.e., three to five students) for discussion to encourage participation from all students.

Online and/or Hybrid Courses

- To use this assignment as a prompt for individual written responses, instruct students to read the following case describing the questioning of an individual. Using what you have learned in your reading and course material, write a one- to two-page response that includes the following:
  - Identification of all aspects of the scenario that are legally relevant and should be considered when determining whether the suspects' statements would be admissible in court. For each aspect, make a "ruling" (or decision) as to whether, in this given case, the aspect would make the statements admissible or inadmissible. Explain why.
  - Of the multiple relevant aspects in the scenarios, determine the issue that is key and explain your reasoning. Include your final decision as to the admissibility of the statements.
  - Assuming this suspect's waiver of *Miranda* rights is under question in the court, what key questions would a forensic evaluator need to assess in evaluating the suspect's capacity? What specific functional abilities would the evaluator examine?
- To use this assignment as a basis for online discussion, create separate conversational threads for each case, using the preceding questions as prompts for students. The debatable nature of many of the issues within the cases should allow students to disagree and weigh various components of the case differently, sparking rich discussion.

REFERENCES   Berghuis v. Thompkins, 130 S. Ct. 2250 (2010).
Brown v. Mississippi, 297 U.S. 278 (1936).
Colorado v. Connelly, 479 U.S. 157 (1986).
Coyote v. United States, 380 F.2d 305 (10th Cir. 1967).

Escobedo v. Illinois, 378 U.S. 478 (1964).

Goldstein, N. E. S., Goldstein, A. M., Zelle, H., & Condie, L. O. (2013). Capacity to waive *Miranda* rights and the assessment of susceptibility to police coercion. In R. K. Otto & I. B. Weiner (Eds.), *Handbook of psychology* (2nd ed., Vol. 11, pp. 381–411). Hoboken, NJ: Wiley.

J.D.B. v. North Carolina, 131 S.Ct. 2394 (2011).

Miranda v. Arizona, 384 U.S. 436 (1966).

Salinas v. Texas, 369 U.S. 176 (2013).

Spano v. New York, 360 U.S. 315 (1959).

10 EVALUATING JUVENILE COMPETENCY TO STAND TRIAL

This activity provides students with the experience of the full forensic mental health evaluation process, including planning an assessment interview, taking notes during an interview, using collateral information and applying the legal standards to the case-specific information. Finally, students write up their findings in a report for the court and are introduced to the challenges of report writing and compiling various sources of information.

LEARNING OBJECTIVES

Students will

(a) gain an understanding of how a competency interview is conducted,
(b) learn how to record interview information in real time,
(c) review and compile multiple sources of data in a forensic mental health assessment, and
(d) demonstrate the ability to write a brief forensic assessment report.

PREPARATION

Prior Didactic Coverage

- This activity should be incorporated after covering forensic mental health assessment and report writing through assigned readings, lectures, or other didactic formats. Students should have a general understanding of the following terms and concepts before engaging in the activity:
  - *Competency to stand trial:* This activity assumes familiarity with the concept of competency to stand trial (CST) but does not require knowledge or experience with the assessment of competency. Psychology and law texts vary in the amount of information provided about CST (see Content Note 10.1). Specialty texts in forensic mental health assessment may be helpful in clarifying key issues and provide relevant readings for instructors or students preparing for this activity (see Kruh & Grisso, 2009; Melton, Petrila, Poythress, & Slobogin, 2007; Stafford & Sellbom, 2013; Zapf & Roesch, 2009).
  - The standard for competency set forth in the *Dusky v. United States* (1960) decision.
  - Frequency and importance of this type of evaluation, including defendants' constitutionally protected right to due process.
  - Because this is a juvenile case, some background information on the juvenile court system may also be helpful but is not required (for a review of CST specific to the juvenile courts, see Kruh & Grisso, 2009).

http://dx.doi.org/10.1037/0000080-011
Activities for Teaching Psychology and Law: A Guide for Instructors, by A. D. Zelechoski, M. Wolbransky, and C. L. Riggs Romaine

Content Note 10.1. *Trial Versus Adjudication*

Although historically called CST, texts may also refer to this evaluation and process as *adjudicative competence*. This terminology acknowledges the need to be competent for the entire adjudicative process (e.g., plea bargaining, decision-making) that is broader than a formal trial. Here, we refer to CST for consistency with commonly used terminology that may be familiar to students.

Materials Needed

- For Phase 1
  - Handout 10.1: Evaluating Juvenile CST Assignment Sheet (one copy for each student)
  - Handout 10.2: Juvenile CST Example Report (one copy for each student or distributed electronically)
  - Handout 10.3: Juvenile CST Report Template (one copy for each student or distributed electronically)
- For Phase 2
  - Video 10.1: Full Juvenile CST Interview (50 minutes); alternatively, Video 10.2: Clinical Interview Only (10 minutes) or Video 10.3: Juvenile CST Interview Only (40 minutes)
  - Handout 10.4: Collateral Documents (one copy for each student or distributed electronically)
- For the instructor:
  - Handout 10.5: Instructor Notes: Interview with Matt (one copy for instructor)
  - Handout 10.6: Juvenile CST Grading Rubric

FACILITATION   This activity typically takes at least two class periods to complete. After necessary prior didactic coverage, the activity can be introduced through Phase 1 (Preparation for the Assessment). Phase 2 (The Interview) can take place the following class session or, if you would like to provide students with more time to prepare for the "interview," during a later class period. When planning this assignment, be sure to provide adequate time for students to write the report between the interview and the report due date.

Phase 1: Preparation for the Assessment

1. Introduce the class to the assignment. Note that students will serve as the evaluators, conducting an evaluation and subsequently writing a report about a young man, Matt, whose attorney referred him for an evaluation of competency to stand trial (see Content Note 10.2).
2. Provide students with the Assignment Sheet, Example Report, and Report Template. Have students fill in the "Important Dates" section in the Assignment Sheet. It will be helpful to provide the report template electronically in a format that students can use as they write their reports (e.g., a Google doc or Microsoft Word document). Many instructors use the course webpage (on Blackboard, Moodle, etc.) as a repository for this type of file and additional reading materials.

Depending on the recency and extent of prior didactic coverage, this may be a helpful time to review the *Dusky* standard and the operational definitions of that standard. A model that considers *understanding, appreciation, ability to assist,* and *decision-making* may be helpful to students as they try to apply the *Dusky* standard and provides an example of how psychologists translate legal standards into psycholegal targets for evaluation (for a review of models, see Kruh & Grisso, 2009). As noted, some states have developed juvenile-specific laws and policies around competency. You may choose to introduce these state-specific criteria for the evaluation process.

3. Lead the class in a discussion to prepare for the "interview." As much as possible, try to put the students in the position of the evaluator, asking them to consider what questions they will ask and what information they will need to obtain. The list that follows provides questions for discussion; much could be discussed for each question. The bullets note key concepts to highlight in discussion. An asterisk (*) denotes topics where you can choose to introduce state- or jurisdiction-specific law about what is required. Specifically, some states have adopted juvenile-specific laws and policies around competency that may provide specific criteria for evaluation. The U.S. Supreme Court decision in *Dusky* is used here as a non–jurisdiction-specific foundation for evaluating CST.

    a. *What information will you need from the attorney?*
       - Information on the charges and offense, including police reports
       - Reports of limitations or problems in the attorney's interactions with Matt
    b. *How will you start the interview?*
       - Consent and limits of confidentiality*
    c. *What do you want to know?*
       - Relevant background information (e.g., developmental history, medical and psychiatric history, education history, social history, general functioning)
    d. *Why do you want to know these things?*
       - Discuss how background information is considered and provides points of comparison for current behavior
    e. *How do you ask about these things?*
       - Have students practice phrasing questions as they would be posed to Matt
    f. *What other sources of information will you want to access?*
       - Discuss the importance of collateral sources in forensic evaluation and what agencies and individuals could serve as helpful collateral sources—in Matt's case, parent, teachers, school records, medical records (*Note.* Although collateral information has been provided in Handout 10.4: Collateral Documents for convenience, you may choose to create additional sources as seen fit on the basis of this class discussion.)
    g. *What specific things do you need to assess for this legal question? How?**
       - Understanding
       - Appreciation
       - Ability to assist council
       - Decision-making
       - Posing hypothetical scenarios to test decision-making

h. *Are there any tools or measures you could use?*
- Juvenile Adjudicative Competence Interview (JACI), structured professional judgment tool for juvenile adjudicative competence

i. *Discuss the practicalities involved:*
- *What if Matt doesn't know something you ask him?*
  - Teach information, test immediate and long-term recollection.
  - *Assessing capacity with teaching*: The evaluation of CST is not simply a test of an individual's legal knowledge. If the defendant does not know the information, his or her *capacity* to learn the information must be evaluated. Especially in evaluations of juvenile defendants, it is quite common for the evaluee not to know information or to be unfamiliar with legal concepts. In these cases, forensic evaluators provide the information (e.g., about the role of the judge) and ask the evaluee for his or her immediate recall. Ideally, evaluators should test the recollection again at the end of the interview or in the next interview to ascertain whether the evaluee can retain the information. Students will see this teaching-and-recall process take place in the interview and may need some explanation as to what is occurring and why.
- *How do you begin the interview?*
  - Discuss building rapport and starting with less threatening or sensitive topics
- *How do you take notes and get all the information down?*
  - Discuss why many lawyers would not let you record this type of interview.
  - Note that, as in real life, students will have one opportunity to get the information Matt provides. Acknowledge that real life allows for follow-up questions, but people do not have rewind buttons, and it is important to practice getting information in real time.
  - Discuss writing versus typing. Some forensic mental health evaluators type their notes during forensic interviews, when feasible. You may choose whether to allow students to bring laptops for taking notes during the "interview." It is important to note that some custodial situations (e.g., prisons or jails) may not allow electronics, and evaluators are sometimes required to conduct evaluations by taking notes on paper.
  - Encourage students to get quotes when possible, and discuss the need to record both questions and answers.
- *How do you put all the information together?*
  - Answer questions about the sample report.
  - Discuss data versus opinions. Note that no new information should be introduced in the opinions section.
- *What if reports do not match?*
  - Discuss dealing with inconsistencies, evaluating sources of information, and noting differences when necessary.

j. *What else will be important to consider while interviewing Matt? Why?*
- Matt's appearance
- Behavioral information obtained from the interview, including his speech, evidence of mental illness, ability to engage and communicate with the interviewer

Phase 2: The Interview

1. In class, show the video interview of Matt provided on the companion website. The full interview is approximately 50 minutes and was designed to simulate the evaluator's perspective, with the focus on the interview subject. There are three versions of the video available on the companion website: the full interview video, the clinical portion of interview only (10 minutes), and the forensic competency portion of interview only (40 minutes); the latter options may be used should you prefer to have students focus on only limited aspects of the interview for this activity.
   - *Viewing the interview video:* Given the amount of information conveyed during the video interview, it is common for students to request to view it multiple times or to have you replay specific parts that they may have missed. Warn students before you start the video that they will only be able to view it once and that they need to take as comprehensive notes as possible. This best simulates the real interview context. In other words, forensic evaluators generally do not have the luxury of recording and playing back or repeating their interviews; thus, they must glean and record as much information as possible from the evaluee during each interview session.
2. After the interview, facilitate a brief discussion. Allow students to ask questions or share observations about the interview. It may be helpful to discuss their observations about his abilities, but avoid discussing whether Matt is competent to stand trial because (a) students may form a premature opinion before reviewing collateral documents and (b) the materials for this activity are designed so that a reasonable argument for competence or incompetence could be made.
3. Hand out the collateral records.
4. Ask whether students have any questions about how to write the report and answer/address concerns accordingly.
   - *Dates in written materials and video interview:* The activity handouts note all dates as X/X/XXXX, and Matt is not asked about his birthdate or the current date in the interview. This is done intentionally to allow the resources to be used over time but may confuse students as they write up the report.
     - It may be helpful to assign real dates in some way. You can create an applicable birthday for Matt (one that would make him 16 at the time of the evaluation) and use the date the interview is shown in class as the interview date. Similarly, current dates could be assigned to collateral materials, or students may be told to note the date as X/X/XXXX.
     - The importance of this issue may vary with the level of the course. In upper-level courses covering forensic assessment in more depth, the forensic assessment principle of attributing information to sources within the report (and dating sources as part of identifying and evaluating sources of information) is likely to have been covered, and you may require students to understand and apply this in their report. In these cases, assigning dates will be useful.

DEBRIEFING   On the date written evaluations are due, allow some time for a full debriefing.

Sample Discussion Questions

- What evidence did you have to suggest Matt was competent?
- What evidence did you have to suggest he was not?
- How did you weigh that evidence, and what did you conclude?
- What was difficult about this assignment?
- What aspects of competency were hardest to assess?
- What unexpected challenges did you encounter?
- What added challenges would there be if you were conducting a real interview?

GRADING   Grading should be based on the content and quality of each student's written juvenile competency evaluation report. In addition to Appendix A: Written Assignment Grading Rubric, which can be modified, as appropriate, an additional grading rubric specific to this assignment is included as Handout 10.6: Juvenile Competency to Stand Trial Grading Rubric.

- As noted earlier, the data available in this case could allow an evaluator to make a reasonable argument that Matt is competent or a reasonable argument that he is not. Reports should be graded not on the conclusion but on the writing clarity, the use of content, the rationale and logic used, and the evidence presented supporting the conclusion.
  - *The ultimate legal question:* Many forensic mental health evaluators would argue that an evaluator should not answer the ultimate legal question (i.e., competence) but should leave that issue for the trier of fact. The sample report (Handout 10.2) is written in keeping with this school of thought and, as such, notes John's abilities and understandings typically considered by the courts when determining competency to stand trial, without directly answering the ultimate legal question. In this assignment, opinions about Matt as simply competent or incompetent are stated in that way for ease and clarity. In upper-level classes or those focusing on forensic assessment, it may be worthwhile to draw students' attention to this issue of answering the ultimate legal question.

MODIFICATIONS   This activity can be modified for the level and time available in a given course. You may choose to assign only some written report sections or to skip the report-writing assignment altogether to allow more time for review and discussion of the interview process and content.

Varying Class Lengths

- Depending on the length of class periods, Phase 1 and Phase 2 can occur on the same day or different days. If necessary, an entire class period may be used to show the interview, with debriefing done during the next class period.

Varying Class Sizes

- This activity can work with any size class with little modification.

Online and/or Hybrid Courses

- Similarly, this activity can easily be used in an online format, with Matt's interview video posted on the course website.
- Discussions and planning for the interview can take place in discussion threads, with students working together to create a list of ideas of questions for Matt. If you do not want students to be able provide students with the ability to watch the interview multiple times, a set time for viewing the video could be assigned.

RESOURCE

Heilbrun, K. (2001). *Principles of forensic mental health assessment.* New York, NY: Kluwer Academic.

REFERENCES

Dusky v. United States, 362 U.S. 402 (1960).

Kruh, I., & Grisso, T. (2009). *Evaluation of juveniles' competence to stand trial.* New York, NY: Oxford University Press. http://dx.doi.org/10.1093/med:psych/9780195323078.001.0001

Melton, G. B., Petrila, J., Poythress, N. G., & Slobogin, C. (2007). *Psychological evaluations for the court: A handbook for mental health professionals and lawyers* (3rd ed.). New York, NY: Guilford Press.

Stafford, K. P., & Sellbom, M. O. (2013). Assessment of competency to stand trial. In R. K. Otto & I. B. Weiner (Eds.), *Handbook of psychology* (2nd ed., Vol. 11, pp. 412–439). Hoboken, NJ: Wiley.

Zapf, P. A., & Roesch, R. (2009). *Evaluation of competence to stand trial.* New York, NY: Oxford University Press. http://dx.doi.org/10.1093/med:psych/9780195323054.001.0001

11   A JOURNEY THROUGH CIVIL COMMITMENT

Civil commitment is a process in which individuals are either voluntarily or involuntarily taken into custody for a prescribed period of time because their mental illness has caused them to be a danger to themselves or others, or because they are so significantly disabled that they cannot properly care for themselves. This often results in a period of hospitalization and psychiatric evaluation. Each state has a series of procedures that must be followed to protect the individual's rights and not unnecessarily restrict individual liberties. This activity is intended to provide students with a glimpse into the various stages of the civil commitment process, including who is involved in decision-making at each stage and how evaluations are conducted.

LEARNING OBJECTIVES

Students will

    (a) describe the steps and sequence of a general civil commitment process (actual processes vary by state), including emergency detention, voluntary inpatient commitment, involuntary inpatient commitment, and outpatient commitment;

    (b) recognize the roles of various providers involved at each stage of the civil commitment process; and

    (c) distinguish between the various methods of assessment to address relevant civil commitment questions.

PREPARATION

Prior Didactic Coverage

- Legal context: State law authorizes the involuntary custody and restraint of an individual who is a danger to self or others or who cannot care for himself or herself due to mental illness.
- Ways to evaluate "dangerousness" and risk
- Civil commitment process: Ideally, provide details about the specific process and requirements in your state (see Resources at the end of this activity).
- Various types of civil commitment: (a) emergency detention, (b) involuntary civil commitment, (c) voluntary civil commitment, and (d) outpatient civil commitment.

Note. See the Resources section at the end of this activity to locate more information on both the general process of civil commitment and state-specific practices.

http://dx.doi.org/10.1037/0000080-012

Activities for Teaching Psychology and Law: A Guide for Instructors, by A. D. Zelechoski, M. Wolbransky, and C. L. Riggs Romaine

Materials Needed

- Handout 11.1: Civil Commitment Process Cards
  - Copy and cut a set of Steps and Players cards for each small group.
  - If possible, make the Steps cards one color and the Players cards another color.
- Handout 11.2: Sample Civil Commitment Process Diagram
- Tape
- Poster board, chalkboard, or wall space to create process diagrams

FACILITATION   Parts 1 and 2 of this activity can be done together in sequence, or either part can be done as a stand-alone activity.

Part 1: Process Diagrams

- Divide the class into small groups (i.e., three to six students).
- Give each small group a set of Civil Commitment Process Cards (i.e., one set of Steps cards and one set of Players cards). Instruct groups that they will have a set period of time (e.g., 2 minutes) to race to put the "Steps" cards in the correct procedural order on the board. Be sure to tell students that they might not use all of the cards, and they can write in additional steps on the blank cards, if they believe a step is missing. Examples of steps include unusual or concerning behavior, brief evaluation, comprehensive evaluation, emergency detention, court hearing, and involuntary inpatient hospitalization. Examples of players include judge, police, concerned citizen, psychologist, psychiatrist, and attorney.
  - *Creating the civil commitment process diagrams:* The civil commitment process can look significantly different across jurisdictions, and as a result, there are many ways to set up these diagrams. This includes both the order of Steps and the Players involved at various steps (i.e., some players are involved in multiple steps). Encourage students to do their best and create an order that reflects what they have read and learned about the civil commitment process.
  - *The "correct" diagram:* See Handout 11.2: Sample Civil Commitment Process Diagram for an example of how the process looks in many jurisdictions. You are encouraged to familiarize yourself with the civil commitment process in your jurisdiction (see Resources at the end of this activity for several state examples). You can use this information to clarify for your students how things work in your local jurisdiction in terms of steps, players, timelines, statutory regulations, civil commitment requirements and definitions, among other factors. If students have not had much exposure to civil commitment as a topic, this activity can be modified to have the didactic components incorporated into the activity in real time (see the Modifications section).
- After the process order is created, instruct students to use their "Player" cards to correctly assign the relevant players to each step in the process (e.g., Judge would be assigned to the Court Hearing step, Psychologist would be assigned to the Comprehensive Evaluation step).
  - *Note.* There are various ways to do this, especially in terms of which roles are assigned to which step (i.e., some roles are involved in multiple steps).

See Handout 11.2: Sample Civil Commitment Process Diagram to see a diagram of a common way this process can flow.

- After the groups have assembled their process diagrams, there are several points for follow-up discussion.
  - Voluntary versus involuntary hospitalization: Most jurisdictions require individuals be allowed to choose voluntary hospitalization, instead of involuntary commitment, at various points in the commitment process. Discussion of these various decision points provides opportunity to discuss the reasoning that underlies the provision of these options and the fundamental liberty issues at stake in the commitment process.
  - Discussion questions about the general process for involuntary hospitalization:
    - Why does the law allow for an emergency detention period? What is required for further commitment?
    - What are the two parts of the legal standard for commitment?
    - Who can petition the court for a professional examination?
    - When are formal hearings conducted? Why? What evidence can the individual in question present?

Part 2: Evaluation Decision-Making

- Using the same small groups from Part 1 (or dividing the class into different groups or pairs—enough groups/pairs to cover each stage), assign each group one Step and the associated Player for the involuntary commitment process. For example, assign one group the Step "Unusual or Concerning Behavior" and the Player "Police" or the Step "Emergency Detention" and the player "Psychiatrist."
- Have each group outline a plan for evaluation and decision-making at that stage.
- Write these sample prompt questions on the board, if desired:
  1. *What are the questions to be addressed by your role?*
     Sample responses:
     a. Police/Mental Health Professional/Citizen: Is the person currently a danger to self or others?
     b. Psychiatrist/Psychologist: Does the person have a mental illness? If so, what is it? Is he or she a danger to self or others? Is he or she gravely disabled or unable to care for basic needs?
     c. Judge: Does the person meet the standard for civil commitment beyond the emergency detention period?
     d. State's Attorney: What is necessary to promote safety in the community? Is this person dangerous and in need of hospitalization?
     e. Patient's Attorney: Is the person mentally ill, dangerous, or gravely disabled? If so, what is the least restrictive alternative? What treatment and supports does this individual need? What is the timeline for reevaluation?
  2. *What methods can you use to address those questions?*
     Sample response categories:
     a. Specific interview questions
     b. Assessment tools
     c. Collateral informants
     d. Records

3. *How much time do you anticipate having to do this assessment?*
   a. Responses would depend on the state's regulations regarding timelines, commitment periods, and so on. Help students distinguish between the time points at which quick decisions are required and time points that allow for thorough evaluation and gathering of information.
4. *What barriers might get in the way of doing your assessment?*
   a. Responses might include factors such as detox or withdrawal symptoms, psychotropic medication side effects, noncompliance, and malingering, for example.

■ Have each group briefly present its evaluation or decision-making plan for their respective step or role.
■ *Incorporating hypothetical scenarios:* In addition to (or instead of) developing a generic evaluation or decision-making plan for Part 2, consider providing students with a specific hypothetical scenario to consider and use as the focus for their decision-making. Examples of common civil commitment scenarios to use include the following:
   ○ A disoriented or aggressive homeless person is picked up by police
   ○ A therapist is in a session with an acutely suicidal client
   ○ A person attacks a family member with a weapon, after experiencing auditory hallucinations commanding him or her to do so
   ○ A person experiencing manic symptoms who is pulled over by the police for reckless speeding and speaks to the officer in a rapid, pressured manner; cannot form coherent sentences; and cannot recall his or her name and address

DEBRIEFING *Sample Discussion Questions*

■ What are some of the differences between criminal incarceration and civil commitment? (See Content Note 11.1.)
■ Which stage of the civil commitment process involves the least comprehensive evaluation? Which stage involves the most comprehensive evaluation?
■ Why might someone opt for voluntary commitment over involuntary commitment?
■ To what extent should this be a legal process, in which a judge makes a commitment determination, versus a clinical process, in which a psychiatric treatment provider makes a commitment determination?

Content Note 11.1. *Criminal Incarceration Versus Civil Commitment*

■ Legally, incarceration falls under the state's police power and civil commitment falls under *parens patriae.*
■ Incarceration is to address past harm; civil commitment is to prevent future harm.
■ Incarceration is focused on punishment; civil commitment is focused on rehabilitation.
■ Process for each is different: Criminal prosecution leading to incarceration includes many legal protections; civil commitment has much fewer protections with respect to due process.
■ Length of commitment differs: with incarceration, there is typically a fixed limit to the sentence; with civil commitment, there may be a limit to each commitment period, but no cumulative limit, and thus the typical length of hospitalizations varies widely.

GRADING Grading should be based on each student's participation and engagement in the activity and his or her use of the available information. To this end, Appendix B: Participation Grading Rubric can be used or modified as needed. Alternatively, or in addition, grading can be based on the content and quality of each student's or group's presentation in Part 2 by using or modifying Appendix C: Presentation Grading Rubric. For group presentations, Appendix D: Group and Self-Evaluation Form can also be used or modified to assess each student's contribution to the overall presentation.

MODIFICATIONS *Varying Class Lengths*

- For shorter class periods, it may not be possible to complete both Parts 1 and 2, or even Part 1 in its entirety. Accordingly, here are some alternative ways to facilitate the activity:
  1. Split Part 1 and Part 2 into two class sessions.
  2. For Part 1, have students race to put just the Steps in order and then facilitate a class discussion in which you add the Players for each Step.
  3. If students have not had much exposure to civil commitment (or did not do their assigned reading!), you can then cover the didactic content while you review their completed diagrams. This may mean talking through why someone may believe an individual needs to be involuntarily hospitalized, who makes that determination, the due process rights of the impaired individual, the difference between a brief and comprehensive evaluation, and the duration of each stage.

Varying Class Sizes

Part 1
- For smaller classes, you can assign each person a Step in the process and then have the students put themselves in what they believe is the correct order, creating a sort of human diagram/flow chart.
- For larger classes, you can assign some small groups the Steps and other small groups the Players, so that all the groups can work simultaneously, while each can focus on a narrower component of the process.

Part 2
- For smaller classes, you can assign each individual a role or step combination and have students work independently to address the prompt questions before reporting their assessment approach to the class.
- For larger classes, you can create small groups and assign each group a role or step combination to address.

Online or Hybrid Courses

Part 1
- Provide students with a list of Steps and Players and have them draw out their diagram (using Microsoft Word, Publisher, or simply on paper) and post a picture of the diagram on the online course platform. After all diagrams have been posted, you can have students engage in a discussion comparing and contrasting

the diagrams, before providing students with your assessment of which diagrams came closest to a typical civil commitment process.

   o Alternatively, you can have students research the civil commitment process in your jurisdiction and instruct them to create a diagram with the Steps and Players you provided that most reflects the process locally. See Resources for several state examples.

   o Alternatively, you can assign each student a different state and have them research the civil commitment process in that state. Instruct students to create and submit a diagram that reflects the process in their assigned state. Students can then compare and contrast the processes in varying states (either through discussion board posts or as a written assignment).

Part 2

- Assign students (either individually or in groups) a Step–Player combination as described and instruct them to post their responses to the prompts listed earlier, describing what the assessment might look like for their particular combination.

- Alternatively, or in addition, assign students a hypothetical case scenario (as discussed in the Facilitation section) on which to base their evaluation or decision-making plan.

RESOURCES   Individual State Statutes and Statistics related to Civil Commitment:

- http://www.treatmentadvocacycenter.org/browse-by-state
- https://mentalillnesspolicy.org/national-studies/state-standards-involuntary-treatment.html

Examples of State Guides to Civil Commitment Process:

- Indiana: https://drive.google.com/file/d/0B00Ao3fD2IK_ZVdxbmFMaEpySlZpSC1NODFFbDI2R1JhdGtj/view
- Maryland: http://namimd.org/uploaded_files/3/What_to_do_in_a_Psychiatric_Crisis_PDF_for_Web.pdf
- Minnesota: http://www.namihelps.org/assets/PDFs/civilcommitmentSinglePg102108.pdf
- Utah: https://dsamh.utah.gov/provider-information/civil-commitment/
- Virginia: http://namivirginia.org/wp-content/uploads/sites/127/2016/03/GuidetoPsychiatricCrisisandCivilCommitmentProcessforWebsite-justlawscriteria2016.pdf

The following may be useful resources as well:

Lareau, C. R. (2013). Civil commitment and involuntary hospitalization of the mentally ill. In R. K. Otto & I. B. Weiner (Eds.), *Handbook of psychology* (2nd ed., Vol. 11, pp. 308–331). Hoboken, NJ: Wiley.

Testa, M., & West, S. G. (2010). Civil commitment in the United States. *Psychiatry*, 7(10), 30–40.

12 DO YOU SWEAR TO TELL THE TRUTH? EXPERT TESTIMONY

The purpose of this activity is to learn about the process of serving as an expert witness or fact witness, specifically in a civil forensic assessment case. Using a hypothetical case summary, students will apply what they have learned about forensic assessment in civil and family law matters by serving as one of several key mental health witnesses in a family law case. In addition to learning about the process, students have the opportunity to serve as either an expert or fact witness and experience the challenge of verbally conveying complex information in an adversarial context.

LEARNING OBJECTIVES

Students will

(a) describe the process of involving expert witnesses in civil matters, particularly in family law-related matters;
(b) distinguish between fact and expert witnesses;
(c) distinguish between direct examination and cross-examination;
(d) identify the purpose for and process of qualifying witnesses;
(e) practice rapid analytical thinking and effective response styles; and
(f) employ strategies used by both attorneys and mental health professionals in legal adversarial contexts.

PREPARATION

Prior Didactic Coverage

- Expert versus fact witness
- Direct versus cross-examination: purpose, types of questions allowed, flow
- Forensic evaluations; specifically, child custody evaluations (e.g., who hires the expert; who is the evaluator's client; evaluation purpose and process; physical vs. legal custody)
  - Alternatively, you may choose to adapt this activity to a forensic evaluation content area already covered in a previous activity (juvenile competence to stand trial, civil commitment, etc.).
- Ethical guidelines related to forensic mental health assessment (e.g., providing testimony about the ultimate legal issue, serving in multiple roles, remaining objective and neutral, etc.)

http://dx.doi.org/10.1037/0000080-013
Activities for Teaching Psychology and Law: A Guide for Instructors, by A. D. Zelechoski, M. Wolbransky, and C. L. Riggs Romaine

Materials Needed

- Handout 12.1: Dr. Casey Smith Materials (copies for half of the students)
- Handout 12.2: Ronnie Dawson Materials (copies for half of the students)
- Handout 12.3: Notes and Sample Questions for Examining Attorney (copies for each participating attorney)
- Furniture needed to arrange classroom as a courtroom (e.g., chair for witness, chair for judge, podium for attorney)

FACILITATION   *Part 1: Assigning Roles; Peer Consultation and Preparation*

- Divide the class into two groups: (a) Dr. Casey Smith and (b) Ronnie Dawson.
  - *Assigning roles:* The names for each role are intentionally unisex to facilitate easier and equitable distribution of students across roles. Because Ronnie Dawson's role is that of a fact witness, this role involves slightly less preparation and mastery of information contained in the materials. If any students in your course might find this activity particularly challenging (for any number of academic or social-emotional reasons), consider assigning those students the role of Ronnie Dawson. For example, it is reasonable to expect some students may exhibit anxiety in response to the anticipation of Part 2.
- Provide each student with the materials appropriate for his or her designated role. Materials include the details of the case relevant to that role, as well as professional background information and credentials.
  - *Timing considerations:* If you plan to do the entire activity (i.e., Parts 1 and 2) in one class session, be sure to assign student roles and disseminate materials before the class session in which you plan to facilitate the activity. Explain to the students that they need to have mastered the content of those materials before the next class session to be prepared to testify. If you plan to split the activity over two or more class sessions, assign the roles and distribute the materials to the students during Part 1 and allow the students time to read through the materials before consulting and strategizing with peers. At the end of that class session, explain to students they need to have mastered the content of those materials before the next class session to be prepared to testify for Part 2.
- Read the following hypothetical case summary to the class:
  - Case Summary: *After several years of emotionally volatile attempts at reconciliation, Mr. and Ms. Jones have filed for divorce and are currently in the midst of a child custody battle regarding their 4-year-old son, Kyle. Given their long, tumultuous history, Judge Wilson ordered a child custody evaluation to get some clarity around issues related to physical and legal custody of Kyle. Dr. Casey Smith conducted the evaluation, submitted a report, and is now being called to testify. In addition, Ms. Jones's therapist, Ronnie Dawson, has also been called to testify.*
- Give students time to consult others in the same role to prepare for testimony. This consultation period should include helping each other anticipate what types of questions will be asked by the attorney and how best to respond.

o *Guiding peer consultation and witness preparation:*
- Circulate among the peer consultation groups and help them anticipate what type of questions they might be asked.
- Are there inconsistencies between their background and credentials and the work they did with the Jones family?
- Do they feel confident in the procedures they used for the evaluation (Dr. Smith) or therapy (Ronnie Dawson)?
- What are their ultimate opinions and why?
- What holes might the attorney try to poke in their testimony?
■ Remind students they are not to share or discuss the information in their materials with any students playing the other role (as this opportunity would not necessarily be possible in an actual case).
■ Explain to the class that, when you reconvene, all students should be prepared to testify if called on to do so.

Part 2: Testimony

■ If possible, arrange the classroom to resemble a courtroom, including a seat for the judge and witness, as well as a podium or seat for the examining attorney. The students waiting to testify or those not selected to testify can sit to the side of the judge and witness seat, appearing like a jury box (although you can explain to students that a jury would not be present for a family law matter such as this).
■ When you are ready to begin the exercise (either during the second half of this class session or during the next class session), decide whether you will have time for all students to testify or just some of the students. Try to involve as many students as is feasible given the class size and amount of time allotted for the exercise.
  o *Selecting students to testify:* Before this class session, put each student's name on a slip of paper; put all the students assigned to one role in a bowl and all the students assigned to the other role in a second bowl to enable random selection and equitable distribution across roles.
    - If you believe you will have enough time for all students to testify for several minutes each, then use the random selection process to determine the order in which students will testify for each role.
    - If you only have time for some students to testify in the allotted time, then estimate how many students you think are feasible to testify in each role and draw that number of students accordingly.
    - In a small class, or if there is only time for three to five students to testify in each role, consider having a group of Ronnie Dawsons or Dr. Smiths take the stand together (seated at a table at the front of the room). This will save some time and allow you to ask each individual a few qualifying questions (ask one student several questions, and then move down the row to the next) and then ask each subsequent student a few direct or cross-examination questions.
    - If any students report a significant amount of anticipatory anxiety or stress related to testifying in front of the class, allow such students the opportunity to complete an alternative (e.g., writing assignment).

- Either you (the instructor) or a guest attorney(s) will play the role of the father's (Mr. Jones's) attorney, which should be explained to the students. Time permitting, the attorney can conduct both direct and cross-examination of Dr. Casey Smith and Ronnie Dawson (see Handout 12.3).
  - *Preparing the examining attorney:* Decide who will play the examining attorney role. Possibilities include you (the instructor), local attorney(s) willing to participate, law students, or faculty colleagues. Before this class session, provide the examining attorney with copies of all of the student materials, as well as Handout 12.3: Notes and Sample Questions for Examining Attorney. Ask the examining attorney to be prepared to be a bit exaggerated in terms of the shift from direct examination to cross-examination and vice versa to highlight the differences in style, purpose, and structure of each line of questioning.
- Before beginning testimony, remind students that they can bring materials with them to "the stand" but that there are pros and cons to consulting those materials during testimony (e.g., confirming the accuracy of one's statements to avoid making an egregious error versus appearing unprepared, hesitant, lacking credibility).
- In addition, remind students there will be times in which they will likely have to "make up" aspects of their responses or go into more detail than was provided in their materials, depending on the questions asked by the attorney. They should feel free to expand on their answers or extrapolate details within their role, but to be careful in doing so, as they may end up contradicting themselves or opening the door to further inquiry.
- Rotate students through testimony and note various responses and issues that come up during the process to discuss in the debriefing period.

DEBRIEFING   Students typically have many reactions, comments, and questions about this activity. Be sure to save time to debrief and answer questions about the content.

Sample Discussion Questions

- How would a real attorney respond?
- Would a judge allow this type of comment?
- Can lawyers ask about that?
- What was the attorney getting at with those questions?
- How did you feel about the experience of testifying?
- Was it challenging to recall so many details?
- Did you feel defensive?
- What types of responses worked well?
- Did you find yourself getting into difficulty at any points?
- What approaches to answering questions were more and less effective (e.g., answering what was specifically asked vs. expanding and providing contextual information)?
- What are the pros and cons of offering an ultimate legal opinion in this case?
- To what extent is an expert's role that of educator versus advocate?
- How can an expert avoid being labeled as a "hired gun"?
- Why is it important for mental health professionals to stay within the bounds of their expertise or particular role in the case? What can happen if they go beyond the scope of their expertise or role?

GRADING Grading should be based on each student's participation and engagement in the activity and his or her preparation and appropriate use of the available information. Appendix B: Participation Grading Rubric can be used or modified for this activity.

MODIFICATIONS *Varying Class Lengths*

- If you need to involve more students or fill more time:
  - Have several students play each role, and ask each student only a few questions before moving on to the next student (i.e., do not ask each student the same questions).
  - Do a direct examination of Dr. Smith or Ronnie Dawson, playing the role of Mom's attorney. In other words, do not do the cross-examination first (playing the role of Dad's attorney). Instead, show how slow, methodical, and collegial direct examination can be (by playing Mom's attorney) and qualify each witness before doing direct examination.

Varying Class Sizes

- For larger classes:
  - If it is not feasible for all students to testify within the time set aside for this activity, it is important to emphasize the random selection component of the activity to ensure all students review the materials and are adequately prepared.
  - You could hold multiple "court" sessions simultaneously to allow more students to testify. To facilitate this, you would need to have several examining attorneys, and you may want to refrain from serving as an examining attorney yourself so that you can circulate among the different "courts" to assess student performance and topics for debriefing discussion.
  - Other ways to incorporate more students include the following:
    - Allow a testifying witness to "phone a friend" and call on a nonselected student to respond to the question.
    - Have the examining attorney occasionally ask another "Dr. Smith" (not currently on the stand) to answer a specific question (to keep everyone engaged).
    - If a witness struggled to respond to a specific question on the stand, during the debriefing segment, ask other students who did not get to testify to try and formulate a response to that challenging question.

Online and/or Hybrid Courses

- For hybrid courses, you can distribute roles and instructions electronically and set up separate discussion boards to allow for peer consultation as described in Part 1. You can then conduct Part 2 in a traditional classroom setting, as described.
- For online courses that have synchronous components, you can distribute roles and instructions electronically and require students to do the peer consultations as described in Part 1, but online. Students can then complete those peer consultations either synchronously (i.e., requiring all students in a peer consultation

group to participate in an online chat in real time) or asynchronously (i.e., setting up the peer consultation as a discussion board and requiring students to post ideas and questions to one another). For Part 2, you could require all students to log in to a chat at the same time and conduct the examination of each witness through a video, audio, or written chat platform.

- For online courses that are exclusively asynchronous, follow the preceding instructions for synchronous courses, and Part 2 could be set up as a set of posted attorney examination questions, to which students are assigned to answer certain questions, depending on their particular assigned role. Answers could be posted in a discussion forum for further class discussion and participation, or answers could be written up and submitted as individual papers.

RESOURCES   Ackerman, M. J., & Gould, J. W. (2015). Child custody and access. In B. L. Cutler & P. A. Zapf (Eds.), *APA handbook of forensic psychology: Vol. 1. Individual and situational influences in criminal and civil contexts* (pp. 425–469). Washington, DC: American Psychological Association.

American Counseling Association. (2014). *ACA code of ethics.* Alexandria, VA: Author. Retrieved from https://www.counseling.org/docs/default-source/ethics/2014-aca-code-of-ethics.pdf?sfvrsn=fde89426_5

American Psychological Association. (2010). Guidelines for child custody evaluations in family law proceedings. *American Psychologist, 65,* 863–867. http://dx.doi.org/10.1037/a0021250

American Psychological Association. (2013). Specialty guidelines for forensic psychology. *American Psychologist, 68,* 7–19. http://dx.doi.org/10.1037/a0029889

American Psychological Association. (2017). *Ethical principles of psychologists and code of conduct* (2002, Amended June 1, 2010 and January 1, 2017). Retrieved from http://www.apa.org/ethics/code/index.aspx

Association of Family and Conciliation Courts. (2006). *Model standards of practice for child custody evaluation.* Retrieved from http://www.afccnet.org/portals/0/modelstdschildcustodyevalsept2006.pdf

Bow, J. N., & Quinnell, F. A. (2004). Critique of child custody evaluations by the legal profession. *Family Court Review, 42,* 115–127. http://dx.doi.org/10.1111/j.174-1617.2004.tb00637.x

Brodsky, S. L. (2007). *Testifying in court: Guidelines and maxims for the expert witness.* Washington, DC: American Psychological Association.

Emery, R. E., Otto, R. K., & O'Donohue, W. T. (2005). A critical assessment of child custody evaluations. *Psychological Science in the Public Interest, 6,* 1–29. http://dx.doi.org/10.1111/j.1529-1006.2005.00020.x

Heilbrun, K. (2001). *Principles of forensic mental health assessment.* New York, NY: Kluwer Academic.

13 CAN WE PREDICT? APPRAISING AND REDUCING RISK

This activity gives students the opportunity to explore the risk assessment and prediction process that can underlie sentencing and release decisions and inform planning of interventions to reduce risk. Students will search the empirical research literature for predictive factors, create questions for inclusion in an assessment, and compare their findings to established tools. The activity provides an opportunity to compare actuarial and structured professional judgment (SPJ) approaches in an applied context and allows students to compare their intuition about risk factors to the empirical findings.

LEARNING OBJECTIVES

Students will

(a) practice consulting and reviewing appropriate sources of information to gain an understanding of risk assessment;

(b) compare and contrast actuarial and SPJ approaches to assessing risk and static and dynamic factors;

(c) identify limitations of risk assessment and the parameters that promote accurate assessment;

(d) experience the challenge of writing clear, specific, and accurate assessment questions for a specific topic; and

(e) practice effective presentation and communication skills.

PREPARATION

Prior Didactic Coverage

- Assessment tools generally
  - In many psychology and law courses, these may have been introduced in the context of common psycholegal assessments, such as evaluation of competency to stand trial (and the established tools in this area).
  - Specifically, students must be aware of the following:
    - Actuarial approaches (those that are scored and include cutoff points)
    - Structured professional judgment approaches (those that provide a framework for considering factors and reaching an evaluative conclusion)
  - Differences between static factors (those that do not change with time or intervention, e.g., age at first offense) and dynamic factors (those that can change with time or intervention, e.g., current substance use)

---

http://dx.doi.org/10.1037/0000080-014
Activities for Teaching Psychology and Law: A Guide for Instructors, by A. D. Zelechoski, M. Wolbransky, and C. L. Riggs Romaine

- Depending on the course and level of student experience, brief information on searching the empirical literature and the use of specialized search engines available at the institution (e.g., PsycINFO, SCOPUS, Academic Search Premier) may also be helpful.

Materials Needed

- Handout 13.1: Sentencing: Risk Assessment Assignment Sheet (one copy for each student)
- Predetermined time parameters for presentations
  - Depending on the time available in class and the number of small groups, determine the time limit for group presentations. Be sure to allow significant time for discussion and comparison to established measures.
  - The assignment sheet (Handout 13.1) assumes students will create visuals (typically PowerPoint or other slides) to go with their presentation. Adjust this requirement as needed for the technology available in the classroom.
- Predetermined topic list: Determine the list of topics you will include, and how groups will receive a topic.
  - *Assignment topics:* You may choose to assign a topic to each group or to allow groups to select a topic of interest.
    - The nature of the assignment allows multiple groups to use the same topic. In fact, this can provide for an interesting point of comparison within later class discussions (e.g., comparing topics each group chose to include and how questions were worded).
    - In considering possible topics, you may choose to limit the range of topics and focus the course on a specific area (e.g., risk for violence) in which you have particular expertise or access to assessment measures.
    - You may also choose to include broader areas of assessing behavior in forensic contexts. This could include topics such as malingering and evaluation of need for involuntary hospitalization.
  - The following list of possible topics includes references to established measures for that topic (see References at the end of the chapter for full names and citations).
    - Violence risk: Violence Risk Appraisal Guide (VRAG; Quinsey, Harris, Rice, & Cormier, 2006), Historical Clinical Risk Management—20, version 3 (HCR–20–V3; Douglas, Hart, Webster, & Belfrage, 2013), Youth Level of Service/Case Management Inventory 2.0 (YLS/CMI; Andrews, Bonta, & Wormith, 2004; Hoge & Andrews, 2011)
    - Risk of future offense/recidivism: YLS/CMI
    - Risk for sexual reoffense: Sexual Violence Risk—20 (SVR20; Boer, Hart, Kropp, & Webster, 1997), Static—99—revised 2003 (Harris, Rhenix, Hanson, & Thornton, 2003).
    - Juvenile violence risk: Structured Assessment for Violence Risk in Youth (SAVRY; Bartel, Borum, & Forth, 2002), YLS/CMI
    - Juvenile risk of future offense/recidivism: SAVRY, YLS/CMI, Early Assessment Risk List for Boys (EARL–B; Augimeri, Koegl, Webster, & Levene, 2001), Early Risk Assessment List for Girls (EARL–G; Levene et al., 2001)

- Juvenile risk for sexual reoffense: Juvenile Sex Offender Assessment Protocol—II (J–SOAP–II; U.S. Department of Justice, 2003), Juvenile Sexual Offense Recidivism Risk Assessment Tool—II (J–SORRAT–II; Epperson, Ralston, Fowers, DeWitt, & Gore, 2006)
  - Test security and copyright limitations may make it difficult or expensive to acquire full copies of the assessment. However, summaries are usually available from the assessment publisher or review chapters. These will generally provide information on the domains assessed and may include sample questions for comparison.
- Preparation for discussion facilitation
  - Between activity Parts 1 and 2, review the established measures for each group's topic.
  - Be prepared to compare and contrast each group's written questions to those included in established measures.
  - To do this, it will be important to know the following about each measure: (a) its approach (actuarial or SPJ), (b) scoring of responses, and (c) sample questions (if possible).

FACILITATION   This activity requires research and preparation by the student small groups. You may choose to provide class time for some of this work, but (in most cases) this activity will need to be divided so that students have several days between Part 1 and Part 2.

- *Assignment timing and depth:* In determining the timing for this assignment, consider the depth and level of preparation expected, and be sure to provide adequate time.
  - This activity can serve as a major course component, with extensive outside research and detailed presentation preparation, or as a brief experiential component of a larger course, requiring less in-depth research and preparation.
  - At a minimum, it is generally helpful to give students a weekend between Parts 1 and 2. Consider giving a week or more between components if students are expected to prepare in detail with their groups. If you are using this as a major course component, you may also choose to increase the number of assessment items written by each group.

Part 1: Assigning Groups and Topics

1. Organize the class into small groups.
2. Assign or allow groups to select a risk assessment or prediction topic.
3. Provide groups with Handout 13.1: Risk Assessment Assignment Sheet and (if possible) time in class to begin preparation with their small groups.
4. Review the assignment components with the class and allow time for questions. Each group is provided the following instructions:
   a. As a group, make your best educated guesses about what will be important to include in a measure assessing your assigned topic. Use your own experiences and knowledge from this and other classes to come up with at least five factors you think will be associated with or predict your assigned topic.

(*Note.* Be sure to record these predictions so you can share them during your class presentation.)

    b. Review the research findings on your topic. Determine what factors have and have not been found to have a relationship or predict your topic.

    c. Using the information you find, write five questions for a measure assessing your topic. In doing so, be sure to determine the following:

        i. How will these questions be delivered (e.g., written self-report format, spoken as part of an interview)?

        ii. How will each question be answered (e.g., open-ended, rated on a scale, assigned a number or category)?

        iii. How will responses be compiled (e.g., Is each item scored? Is there a total score? Are any questions given more weight?)?

        iv. What is your tool's approach? (e.g., Is it an actuarial tool? SPJ?)

5. Prepare a ____ minute presentation to deliver in class on _____. You should present the information both visually and verbally, and include the following:

    a. Your initial educated guesses about predicting factors.

    b. Your five questions and descriptions of each. Include the evidence you found supporting each factor in the literature, and your answers to the preceding questions about how questions are delivered, scored, and compiled.

    c. Your reasoning for the approach and style of your questions.

    d. A comparison of what you expected your tool to include and what factors you ended up including.

Part 2: Presentation and Class Discussion

1. Allow the first group to give their presentation to the class.

    ■ *Overlapping topics:* If more than one group researched the same topic or if groups' topics overlap, consider when discussion will be most fruitful. You may choose to let each group present, then hold a general discussion comparing and contrasting the different approaches. Similarly, if groups researched juvenile and adult risk assessment, you may want to lead a discussion after both topics are presented to allow for comparison.

2. Lead a class discussion about the topic, challenging each group to think flexibly about their topic and compare it with established measures.

    ■ General follow-up questions

        ○ Which of your factors are static? Which are dynamic?

        ○ What made you choose this approach?

        ○ How did you determine how questions would be delivered (and why)?

        ○ What factors were you surprised by? What were you surprised was *not* associated with your topic?

        ○ Can you identify any challenges to administering this measure as planned? Would it be challenging to get reliable information?

        ○ *If information is gathered only from the individual being assessed*: Would the person being assessed be able to "fake good" or give "right" answers? Would he or she be likely to do so in this context?

- *Comparison to established measures* (Provide the class with information about established measures of their topic. Include sample questions if possible.)
  - ○ Does the established measure take the same approach as the group? Why do you think this may be?
  - ○ What similarities or differences do you see in the approaches?
  - ○ (To the group) Do any aspects of the established measure surprise you, given your research?
3. Repeat this process until all groups have presented their findings to the class.
4. Conclude with a cross-topic comparison of the approaches taken by both the groups and the established tools reviewed. Have students consider and discuss the following:
   - ▪ Why are different approaches taken for different topics?
   - ▪ What are the similarities across topics?
   - ▪ Do any tools or topics seem to require a unique approach?
   - ▪ What are the limits of each measure or approach?

DEBRIEFING   Lead the class in a brief discussion of this process.

Sample Discussion Questions

- ▪ Did you run into unexpected challenges?
- ▪ Was there much literature available on your topic?
- ▪ What challenges did you encounter in trying to write good questions?

GRADING   Grading should be based on the content and quality of each student's or group's presentation. Appendix C: Presentation Grading Rubric can be used and/or modified for this activity. For group presentations, Appendix D: Group and Self-Evaluation Form can also be used or modified to assess each student's contribution to the overall presentation. In evaluating each group's presentation, consider the feasibility of each group's approach and their use of the literature and research findings as a basis for their questions.

- ▪ Additional elements to evaluate include the following:
  - ○ points for addressing each required element,
  - ○ use of slides and clarity of material presented,
  - ○ use of literature, and
  - ○ ability to provide rationale and explain reasoning.

MODIFICATIONS   *Varying Class Lengths*

- ▪ If the time available in class for presentations is limited, you may choose to limit the number of topics covered (e.g., have all groups examine violence risk assessment) and save discussion and comparison to established measures for the end of the session after all groups present.
- ▪ Alternatively, you could require students to write up the same material, instead of doing in-class presentations.

Varying Class Sizes

- For larger classes, it may be difficult to accommodate the number of small group presentations. The modifications described for class length may be helpful.
- Very large classes may be broken into large groups (made up of several small groups), and presentations could occur within these large groups or established discussion or lab sections with teaching assistants monitoring some sections.

Online and/or Hybrid Courses

- This activity can be assigned in a similar manner to individuals or groups online.
- Presentations can be created and submitted using the feature available in most presentation programs (e.g., PowerPoint) that allows audio to be recorded over a presentation.
- Students can be required to post their presentations, watch all other student group presentations, and post a written response or reaction to a certain number of group presentations (e.g., at least two other presentations).
  o Depending on the structure of the course and the student population, it may be challenging for students to work in groups online.
  o This activity could be assigned to individuals or used as a prompt for written responses.
  o If you choose to use the small-group format online, be sure to leave enough time for students to connect and communicate about the project.
  o You should encourage small groups to first and foremost decide what method of communication works best for them (e.g., class discussion board, group texts, e-mail) and take into account the fact that it will often take students a few days to make this decision or plan. It is therefore suggested that at least an additional week be provided for groups to communicate and work on group projects online, compared with the in-person class context.

REFERENCES   Andrews, D. A., Bonta, J., & Wormith, S. (2004). *The Level of Service/Case Management Inventory user's manual*. North Tonawanda, NY: Multi-Health Systems.

Augimeri, L. K., Koegl, C. J., Webster, C. D., & Levene, K. S. (2001). *Early Assessment Risk List for Boys (EARL–B)*, Version 2. Toronto, Ontario, Canada: Earl's Court Child and Family Centre.

Bartel, P., Borum, R., & Forth, A. (2002). *Structured Assessment for Violence Risk in Youth (SAVRY)*. Tampa: Florida Mental Health Institute, University of South Florida.

Boer, D. P., Hart, S. D., Kropp, P. R., & Webster, C. D. (1997). *The manual for the Sexual Violence Risk—20: Professional guidelines for assessing risk of sexual violence*. Vancouver, British Columbia, Canada: British Colombia Institute Against Family Violence.

Douglas, K. S., Hart, S. D., Webster, C. D., & Belfrage, H. (2013). *HCR–20V3: Assessing risk of violence—User guide*. Burnaby, British Columbia, Canada: Mental Health, Law, and Policy Institute, Simon Fraser University.

Epperson, D. L., Ralston, C. A., Fowers, D., DeWitt, J., & Gore, K. S. (2006). Actuarial risk assessment with juveniles who offend sexually: Development of the Juvenile Sexual Offense Recidivism Risk Assessment Tool—II. In D. Prescott (Ed.), *Risk *assessment of youth who have sexually abused: Theory, controversy, and emerging strategies* (pp. 118–169). Oklahoma City, OK: Wood & Barnes.

Harris, G. T., Rhenix, A., Hanson, R. K., & Thornton, K. (2003). *Static–99 coding rules revised—2003*. Ottawa, Ontario, Canada: Department of the Solicitor General of Canada.

Hoge, R. D., & Andrews, D. A. (2011). *Youth Level of Service/Case Management Inventory 2.0 (YLS/CMI 2.0): User's manual*. Toronto, Ontario, Canada: Multi-Health Systems.

Levene, K. S., Augimeri, L. K., Pepler, D. J., Walsh, M. M., Webster, C. D., Koegl, C. J., & Webster, C. D. (2001). *Early Risk Assessment List for Girls—Version 1* (consultation ed.). Toronto, Ontario, Canada: Earl's Court Child and Family Centre.

Quinsey, V. L., Harris, G. T., Rice, M. E., & Cormier, C. A. (2006). *Violent offenders: Appraising and managing risk* (2nd ed.). Washington, DC: American Psychological Association. http://dx.doi.org/10.1037/11367-000

U.S. Department of Justice, Office of Justice Programs, & Office of Juvenile Justice and Delinquency Prevention. (2003). *Juvenile Sex Offender Assessment Protocol—II (J–SOAP–II) manual*. Washington, DC: Author.

14 FREEZE! WHAT'S A JUVENILE JUSTICE FACILITY TO DO?

■ ─── ■

The purpose of this activity is to expose students to common scenarios that often arise in juvenile justice facilities and have them conduct research to determine what types of responses or interventions are most supported by the empirical literature. Students will be assigned a hypothetical scenario and will serve as juvenile justice consultants with expertise in evidence-based practices. They are tasked with reviewing the literature and developing specific recommendations for the juvenile justice facility to address the situation using best practices.

■ ─── ■

LEARNING OBJECTIVES

Students will

(a) describe common situations and issues that arise in juvenile justice facilities,
(b) recognize the necessary elements of evidence-based practices in juvenile justice,
(c) identify and describe potential interventions and responses to common juvenile justice scenarios using evidence-based practice principles, and
(d) construct a rationale for specific juvenile justice recommendations.

PREPARATION

Prior Didactic Coverage

- Juvenile justice system, including the following:
  o rehabilitation (as opposed to punishment) mandate of most juvenile justice systems;
  o diversion, probation, and community-based alternatives to secure detention available in the juvenile justice system; and
  o high prevalence of mental health disorders and trauma exposure among delinquent youth.
- Evidence-based practice (EBP), including the following:
  o Generally speaking, EBP is the "integration of best research evidence with clinical expertise and patient values" (Sackett, Straus, Richardson, Rosenberg, & Haynes, 2000, p. 1).
  o "As applied to the juvenile justice arena, [EBP] refers generally to programs, practices, and policies used to prevent and reduce youth crime that have been documented to be effective through rigorous evaluation" (Juvenile Justice Information Hub, n.d.).

http://dx.doi.org/10.1037/0000080-015
Activities for Teaching Psychology and Law: A Guide for Instructors, by A. D. Zelechoski, M. Wolbransky, and C. L. Riggs Romaine

○ Rigorous evaluation typically includes a controlled experimental study in which youth are randomly assigned to a treatment or control condition to test the effectiveness of the intervention. It may be helpful to discuss with students what would and would not be considered empirical support for an intervention.

Materials Needed

- Handout 14.1: Student Instructions (copies for all students)
- Handout 14.2: Juvenile Justice Scenarios (each scenario should be copied for the number of students to whom that scenario is assigned)

FACILITATION *Prior Class Session*

- In a class session before the session in which the activity is to take place, divide the class into small groups (i.e., three to six students per group). This activity can also be completed by students individually (as described later in the activity).
- Provide all students with a copy of Handout 14.1.
- Present each group with one of the hypothetical scenarios described in Handout 14.2.
  ○ *Considerations for selecting and assigning scenarios:* Some of the hypothetical scenarios raise issues that have more robust bodies of empirical research available than others. Consider the number of scenarios needed for your class, and determine whether to focus on those with more extensive bodies of research or to include some less researched topics as well. If less researched topics are included, it may be helpful to discuss these limitations with those groups and talk with them about how empirically supported techniques can be generalized to other groups' topics. Some of the hypothetical scenarios raise controversial societal, systemic, or policy issues. Depending on the size and nature of the course, it may be helpful to give students the option to "trade" topics, if needed. You may also choose to exclude some topics based on the course structure (e.g., online vs. in person), campus culture, or other relevant factors.
  ○ *Timing considerations*: The time allotted to the activity can and should vary based on the weight given to the activity, and the level of research and preparation expected. This activity can be used as a significant course component, in which case groups and topics should be assigned several weeks before presentations will be given in class. To use this activity as a smaller course component, topics could be assigned one or two class periods before presentations, ensuring that adequate time is provided for literature review.
- Go through Handout 14.1 with all students, explaining the activity parameters and the written summary expectations.
  ○ Explain to students that they will need to conduct some research on best practices to determine what juvenile justice staff should do to respond to the particular scenario assigned.
  ○ Each student or group must prepare a brief written summary (including references list) explaining their recommendations and empirical rationale for these recommendations and turn in that summary at the beginning of the class on the day of the activity.

Activity Class Session

- Have each group present its scenario and its findings and recommendations for how juvenile justice staff should handle the situation.
  - *Individual student activity:* If you prefer to have this be a primarily individual exercise, assign different scenarios to each student and instruct the students to conduct their research and prepare their written summaries individually. On the day of the activity, you can have students either present their recommendations to the class individually or grouped with the other students who were assigned the same scenario. If you opt to group students according to scenario, have them come together in small groups (organized by scenario) at the beginning of the class session to compile their findings and come up with a unified set of recommendations to present to the class.
- A possible presentation format could include the following:
  - Read the scenario.
  - Present a brief overview of the relevant empirical research on the issue(s) presented in the scenario.
  - Explain the recommendations and rationale for recommendations made to juvenile justice staff for how to handle the scenario.
- If you want the students to be particularly active in this exercise, you could incorporate a role-play or acting component in which the students role-play their scenario and subsequent recommendations. This may be particularly helpful in upper-level courses or in courses targeting clinical or applied students. This format allows the students to face the inherent challenges of actually doing the recommendations, as opposed to just stating what should be done. A sample format could include (a) role-playing the original scenario or (b) having "time-outs" or "freeze" spots, where the students then insert their alternate EBP (evidence-based practice) endings or recommendations. Then have a debriefing discussion in which students provide an overview of the empirical rationale for their specific recommendations and interventions.

DEBRIEFING   Depending on the scenarios used, debriefing may be particularly important for this activity.

Sample Discussion Questions

- What challenges did you face in responding to your scenarios?
- How likely do you think each of these scenarios are in the real world?
- How do you think juvenile justice facilities typically respond to each of these scenarios?
- On the basis of your research, what empirical support did you find supporting your particular intervention or recommended response strategy?
- What challenges do you think juvenile justice staff would face in implementing your recommendations?
- What challenges do you think juvenile justice staff face when trying to use EBPs in their systems and facilities? Examples could include the following:
  - Limited resources
  - Limited staff

      ◦ Limited reinforcements or incentives
      ◦ Lack of training opportunities
      ◦ Lack of buy-in from higher level administration

GRADING

Grading should be based on the content and quality of each student's or group's presentation. Appendix C: Presentation Grading Rubric can be used or modified for this activity. For group presentations, Appendix D: Group and Self-Evaluation Form can also be used or modified to assess each student's contribution to the overall presentation.

Alternatively, or in addition, the written assignment component of the activity can be graded (either individually or each group given a grade for their written summary) and Appendix A: Written Assignment Grading Rubric used or modified as appropriate.

MODIFICATIONS

Varying Class Lengths

- For shorter time periods, consider conducting this activity in one class session as more of a quick think tank or brainstorming format. Assign groups and scenarios as already described, and give groups a brief period of time in class to come up with the recommendations. If desired and feasible, you could require students to bring computers to class so that quick online research can be done during this brainstorming process to review EBPs for various scenarios.
- To conduct this activity without using a small group format (which also takes less time), you can print each scenario on a large poster-sized sheet of paper and post them in different places around the room. Pass out a set of sticky notes to each student and ask them to jot down potential recommendations for each scenario and then post them anonymously on that scenario's poster. Designate a set period of time for students to do this and then reserve some time to facilitate a discussion that not only debriefs the activity (see the preceding sample discussion questions) but also incorporates discussion regarding whether and to what extent the students' recommendations are consistent with EBPs and empirical research.
- For longer class periods or to spread the activity over multiple class sessions, you can allow for preparatory discussions during multiple class sessions. For example, you could allow students to do some initial brainstorming about potential solutions during the first class session, instruct them to go and do individual research on EBP, and then provide time in a second class session for students to report back to their groups about whether their initial solutions and recommendations were consistent with the empirical literature. You can also spread the group presentations and debriefing discussions over multiple class sessions.

Varying Class Sizes

- For smaller classes, you can make this an individual exercise, rather than a group exercise, and assign students different scenarios. Even if multiple students are assigned the same scenario, they are likely to come up with different recommendations, which makes for interesting debriefing discussions.
- For larger classes, you can assign multiple small groups the same scenario and, in lieu of each group presenting, have the groups come together with the other groups assigned to the same scenario and collectively decide on their top three

recommendations. Each combined scenario group can then report to the class their final recommendations and associated empirical rationale.

Online or Hybrid Courses

- You can assign this as either an individual or group activity and require students or groups to post a brief summary of their recommendations and empirical rationale in response to their assigned scenario.
- You can also set up discussion boards for each scenario or for the overall activity to address some of the debriefing questions.

RESOURCES　Lipsey, M. W., Howell, J. C., Kelly, M. R., Chapman, G., & Carver, D. (2010, December). *Improving the effectiveness of juvenile justice programs. A new perspective on evidence-based practice.* Washington, DC: Center for Juvenile Justice Reform, Georgetown University. Retrieved from http://cjjr.georgetown.edu/wp-content/uploads/2015/03/ImprovingEffectiveness_December2010.pdf

Office of Juvenile Justice and Delinquency Prevention. (n.d.). *Model programs guide.* Retrieved from http://www.ojjdp.gov/mpg

REFERENCES　Juvenile Justice Information Hub. (n.d.). *Evidence-based practices: Glossary.* Retrieved from http://jjie.org/hub/evidence-based-practices/glossary

Sackett, D. L., Straus, S. E., Richardson, W. S., Rosenberg, W., & Haynes, R. B. (2000). *Evidence-based medicine: How to practice and teach EBM* (2nd ed.). Edinburgh, Scotland: Churchill Livingstone.

15 PROBLEM SOLVED? CREATING A PROBLEM-SOLVING COURT

This activity is intended to enhance students' exposure to alternative adjudication and correctional formats used within the criminal justice system. Problem-solving courts divert offenders with specific issues away from the typical criminal trial process to address a specific emotional, behavioral, or systemic issue. The rationale is that by addressing the underlying issue, such as drug use or mental illness, the criminal behavior and likelihood of recidivism will be significantly decreased, which will also reduce the resources required of the criminal justice system. Students will use existing research to identify a relevant problem associated with offending and design a problem-solving court to address that issue.

LEARNING OBJECTIVES

Students will

(a) recognize the importance of problem-solving courts as an alternative to incarceration;
(b) analyze the notion that by addressing the causal factor, criminal behavior can be decreased;
(c) compare and contrast the differences in procedure between the typical criminal trial process and problem-solving courts;
(d) engage in critical thinking to determine what causal factors, if addressed by a problem-solving court, could affect recidivism rates; and
(e) creatively develop an alternative process to the typical trial process and incarceration.

PREPARATION

Prior Didactic Coverage

To complete this activity, students will need a basic understanding of the theory and process of problem-solving courts. Prior coverage should include the following:

- overview of the typical criminal trial process;
- history of the development and purpose of problem-solving courts, including the intent to directly address the underlying cause of criminal behavior, as well as outcomes showing the effectiveness of such courts;
- the development and evolution of drug courts (*Note.* Drug courts are a helpful example of a problem-solving court because there is a substantial body of research documenting their development and effectiveness); and

---

http://dx.doi.org/10.1037/0000080-016
Activities for Teaching Psychology and Law: A Guide for Instructors, by A. D. Zelechoski, M. Wolbransky, and C. L. Riggs Romaine

- other examples of problem-solving courts: mental health court, veterans court, homeless court, domestic violence court, and community court.

Materials Needed

- Handout 15.1: Create a Problem-Solving Court Worksheet (one copy for each student)
- Examples of problem-solving courts (using local examples may be helpful and interesting; information about such programs is typically accessible through your state or county government websites)
- Video or newspaper article(s) discussing a timely problem-solving court success or current event
- Predetermined small group assignments or chosen format in which to divide students into small groups (i.e., three to six students per group)
- If making flowcharts or diagrams, provide necessary materials (e.g., paper, scissors, tape)

FACILITATION   This activity is designed to take place over the course of two class periods, with sufficient time in between for small groups (or individual students) to work on developing their own problem-solving court. During the first class session, students are placed into groups and the activity instructions are provided. Each small group will then present their problem-solving court during the second class period. If time permits, allow small groups in-class time to work on this activity (either on the first day or during a later class session, after small groups have had time to work on the activity outside of class).

During Class 1

1. Explain the activity to the class, including goals and grading structure.
   - Sample language: "Create your own problem-solving court that focuses on an underlying or specific issue that, when adequately addressed, might also decrease the likelihood that someone would engage in future criminal behavior."
2. Divide the class into small groups (i.e., three to six students). Each group will be working together over the designated period of time to create and develop their own problem-solving courts. Because both drug courts and mental health courts are now commonly found across the country and have a substantial body of literature highlighting their structure, process, and effectiveness, consider using these types of courts as examples rather than allowing students to use them as the bases for their own courts.
3. Specific instructions to students are as follows:
   - Choose a specific need or problem that has been shown to lead to criminal behavior or that you believe may do so.
   - Find empirical research in the social science literature to support your choice. You will need to explain (during the oral presentation or in a written report) why that specific need or problem was chosen by citing empirical sources that

establish a relationship between your identified problem and future offending/recidivism or criminal behavior.

- Develop the problem-solving court. Depending on the specific issue chosen, each court may function somewhat differently in terms of procedures and goals.
- As you design your court, consider these questions:
  - What are the characteristics of the people being diverted into this court?
  - What goals (related to the issue/problem chosen) will the court want participants to meet (e.g., in a drug court, abstinence or sobriety might be a goal)? In what amount of time?
  - What resources will participants need to meet these goals? For example: Do members of this group need treatment? Do they need assistance with housing, employment, vocational training, or other concerns? Should other people, such as family members, be involved?
  - Who is best suited to assist participants through this process? Who should be involved in the problem-solving court (e.g., social worker, doctor)?
  - What would be the best process to track these goals and progress made? For example:
    1. How often should the person return to court?
    2. How will the court know that the person has made progress (e.g., reports generated from treatment, letter from employer, self-report)?
    3. Should a single judge or more than one person preside over the court?
  - What are the consequences if someone does not meet his or her goals within a certain amount of time?
- Create a presentation that outlines your problem-solving court. Include the process for a participant in the court, including goals, the process of evaluating completion of goals, and consequences for failure to complete goals. Present your court to the class. This could include a PowerPoint presentation, video, and/or flowchart or diagram of how the court will run.
- *Optional*: You may want to have students use only one presentation format or medium. You may also want to require students to submit written descriptions of their problem-solving courts (see the Online and/or Hybrid Courses section for an example of what to ask students to include).

Have students present their problem-solving courts during Class 2.

DEBRIEFING   After all groups have presented their problem-solving courts to the class, review the purpose and goals of this assignment and discuss students' overall experience.

Sample Discussion Questions

- How did you choose the type of problem-solving court you developed? Was it difficult? Were there other issues you also wanted to include or were interested in focusing on in a different way?
- What were the similarities across the various courts created by the class? Were there important differences in approaches? Why or why not?
- Do you see these courts as opportunities or punishment?

- What challenges did you or your group face while developing the court?
- A common constraint systems face is economics. Courts need to find the money to develop these specialty courts. If you are a policymaker, how do you decide which groups should have the option of being diverted from the typical process and afforded an opportunity to participate in a problem-solving court?
- Were any of your personal views affected by this exercise?

GRADING

Grading should be based on the content and quality of each student or group presentation. Appendix C: Presentation Grading Rubric can be used or modified for this activity. For group presentations, Appendix D: Group and Self-Evaluation Form can also be used or modified to assess each student's contribution to the overall presentation.

For example, each grade could be calculated based on the following:

- Group Work
  - How the problem-solving court focus was chosen (i.e., exhibiting evidence that the group researched and chose an empirically-supported causal factor on which to focus the court)
  - Presentation of the court (e.g., content, organization, level of effort exhibited)
  - Written description of the court (i.e., content, format, requirements)
  - Written flowchart of the court process (i.e., completion, level of effort exhibited)
- Individual Work
  - Observations of individual student during the group oral presentation and while observing other presentations (e.g., engaged, respectful)
  - You may choose to add an individual component, such as a journal entry, reflection paper, or short essay about the project and the student's experience

MODIFICATIONS

Varying Class Lengths

- If time permits, provide students the opportunity to work on the project during class time.
  - In-class time is most beneficial after small groups have had some time to work together on the project outside of class.
  - Ask students to come to this class period prepared with their chosen problem-solving court issue and research related to the selected topic.
  - Allowing students in-class small group time has many benefits. Small groups have a set time when they work on the assignment. This helps ensure they are on track according to the activity timeline, especially if you require that they come to class prepared with background research already conducted.
  - Check in on each group's progress, answer any questions that arise, guide the group toward the activity goals, and observe group dynamics and participation among group members.
- If a flowchart is part of this assignment, you should bring any necessary materials to this class session (e.g., paper, markers, scissors).

- If time does not allow each group to present their court to the class, a writing assignment alone could be used as an alternative format to summarize each group's design.

Varying Class Sizes

- Small group sizes can be adjusted for class size. However, groups should be kept to a maximum of six students.
- If the class is too small for group work, this can be an individual assignment in which students are asked to create their own presentation or written summary.

Online and/or Hybrid Courses

- Small groups can work together and post their final product to the online classroom.
  - You can provide more concrete requirements for these final products (e.g., the types of information that must be covered, the format, whether an auditory or visual component should be included).
  - After the final problem-solving courts are posted, have students review each other's design and engage in discussions about their respective court designs.
  - Set specific requirements for how many comments must be posted by each student by certain due dates.
- Students can create a written summary to be submitted (in addition to or in lieu of the posted presentation). For example, instruct students to submit the following:
  1. Name your court (can be as creative as you would like).
  2. Explain the specific need or problem the court will address. Explain why it is important to develop a problem-solving court around this need. In this section, cite to the source(s) you found in correct American Psychological Association style citation format.
  3. List and explain the goals set for people being diverted from the criminal justice system through this court.
  4. Explain how the issue chosen will be addressed or treated. For example, will the diverted persons receive specific treatment, trainings, housing? Will they be assigned a person or a team to help them through this process (e.g., a social worker, doctor)? You are encouraged to conduct scholarly research to help you complete this section and to support why you are recommending this course of action.
  5. Develop a procedure for how the court will be conducted. For example, is there only one judge, how long does a person stay involved in the court, who decides whether a person has completed the court successfully, and what happens if a person does or does not complete the course of action or treatment?
  6. Explain how this court is different from the typical criminal trial process.
  7. Write a brief reflection on your experience developing this court. For example, was it more or less challenging than expected? Did it affect your views of the court or trial process?

RESOURCES Berman, G., & Feinblatt, J. (2001). Problem-solving courts: A brief primer. *Law & Policy,* *23,* 125–140.

Center for Court Innovation. (n.d.). *Problem-solving justice.* Retrieved from http://www.courtinnovation.org/topic/problem-solving-justice

National Association of Drug Court Professionals. (n.d.). *Problem-solving courts: Addressing a spectrum of issues.* Retrieved from http://www.nadcp.org/learn/what-are-drug-courts/types-drug-courts/problem-solving-courts

16 MAY IT PLEASE THE COURT: AMICUS CURIAE BRIEF

In this activity, students are tasked with writing their own amicus curiae briefs for the court. These briefs are often written by interested third parties and submitted to an appellate court in an attempt to influence the trier of fact. Students will learn about the amicus curiae process, purpose, and format and will then choose a topic on which to submit their own brief.

This activity can serve as a major writing assignment for the course. It is suggested that you carefully review this assignment at the start of the term and provide due dates for each step of the process. This scaffolding provides accountability, structure, and the ability to ensure that students understand the assignment details because it is likely the first time they will have heard of and read, let alone written, an amicus brief.

LEARNING OBJECTIVES

Students will

(a) gain and apply in-depth knowledge of a specific area of psychology and the law,
(b) develop and demonstrate persuasive writing skills,
(c) use and demonstrate an ability to synthesize and evaluate knowledge, and
(d) learn and apply correct American Psychological Association (APA) Style citation format.

PREPARATION

Prior Didactic Coverage

- Overview of the typical trial process (specifically how a case goes from the trial level to the appellate level courts)
- Overview of amicus curiae brief process: purpose, who writes them, and how the court uses them to make decisions (see Content Note 16.1)
- The difference between a court affirming or overturning a previous decision (and how this relates to the amicus curiae brief process)

Materials Needed

- Handout 16.1: Overview of Amicus Curiae Brief Assignment (one copy for each student; insert your own due dates, page length, and empirical source requirements)
- Sample amicus curiae brief (one copy for each student or posted electronically)
  o Sample amicus briefs can easily be found online. For example, amicus briefs submitted by the APA on issues can be accessed at http://www.apa.org/about/

http://dx.doi.org/10.1037/0000080-017
Activities for Teaching Psychology and Law: A Guide for Instructors, by A. D. Zelechoski, M. Wolbransky, and C. L. Riggs Romaine

- Defined by *Black's Law Dictionary* (Black & Nolan, 2014): *amicus curiae*. (ə-mee-kəs kyoor-ee-ee) [Latin "friend of the court"] A person who is not a party to a lawsuit but who petitions the court or is requested by the court to file a brief in the action because that person has a strong interest in the subject matter.
- An amicus curiae brief is prepared by an individual, group, organization, or combination of these and provides information about the potential results or impact of a decision.
- The U.S. Supreme Court rules require that the brief covers "relevant matter" not dealt with by the parties in the case that "may be of considerable help" in the court's decision-making process (Supreme Court Rules, Part VII, Rule 37(1), 2013). The brief should identify which party the brief is supporting or whether the brief supports affirmance or reversal of the lower court's decision.

offices/ogc/amicus/index-issues.aspx. The APA has submitted amicus briefs on many topics typically covered in psychology and law courses. Consider using an APA amicus brief as a class reading to introduce the format and structure of briefs to the class.

FACILITATION
Students will likely work on this paper throughout a large portion of the term. Early in the course, you should introduce the topic of amicus curiae briefs and review the assignment carefully (including due dates and expectations throughout the term). Once the assignment has been reviewed, you will need to revisit aspects of this assignment as due dates approach.

It is suggested that different parts of the assignment are due throughout the term, each building on the next. Such scaffolding could be broken down as follows:

1. *Paper topic:* Topic selection should be an enjoyable part of this assignment. Students have two options for how to go about topic selection: (a) they can find a specific court case of interest or (b) they can research and choose an area of psychology and the law that interests them, then find a related case.
   - Once students have chosen their cases, they must decide which party they support. The amicus brief will be written with the intent to convince the court to decide the case in that party's favor. The amicus brief will argue that the court should either affirm or overturn the lower court's decision. It is suggested that students begin developing their topic early in the term and are required to submit their topic for approval within the first quarter of the term. Assist students who are having difficulty finding a case or topic of interest, or help guide them in choosing a perspective around which to form the paper's arguments.
2. *Paper outline and reference page:* To assist students with argument development and effective time management, a second due date requires students to submit an outline and reference page draft (in correct APA format). You may choose to require a certain number of empirical sources (e.g., peer-reviewed journal articles) be included in the paper. This assignment component provides students with the opportunity to focus on this requirement and gives you the opportunity to clarify any confusion or difficulties if needed.
3. *Comprehensive first draft:* Similar to the paper outline, having students submit a full first draft provides another layer of organization and time management.

If time permits, this could be an opportunity for partner or small group work in which students are required to read each other's drafts and provide supportive, helpful feedback to one another. This should be due at least 2 weeks before the final paper due date.

4. *Final paper:* Typically, this is due toward the end of the term.

DEBRIEFING   On the day the final paper is due (or later, if needed), discuss students' thoughts and experiences writing an amicus brief.

Sample Discussion Questions

- How did you go about choosing your case or your perspective?
- What challenges did you experience throughout this assignment?
- Was it difficult to write to the court in a persuasive way?
- Were any of your personal views affected by this assignment?

GRADING   Grading should be based on the content and quality of each student's written amicus curiae brief. In addition to Appendix A: Written Assignment Grading Rubric, which can be modified and used, as appropriate, an additional grading rubric specific to this assignment is included as Handout 16.2: Sample Amicus Curiae Brief Grading Rubric.

MODIFICATIONS   *Varying Class Lengths*

- Consider class length when assigning due dates. The amount of research required (i.e., the number of sources) and the amount of scaffolding can be varied to fit the course length.

Varying Class Sizes

- This assignment should not be affected by class size unless you choose to place students in small groups or with partners at any point in the scaffolding process.
- However, in extremely large classes, the assignment could be modified to be a group assignment in which small groups work together to write and submit an amicus curiae brief.

Online and/or Hybrid Courses

- This assignment requires little modification for hybrid or entirely online courses.
- You can follow the suggested facilitation as detailed above in an online environment. Using small group work is even more beneficial for online courses.
- Two modifications could be as follows:
  ○ During the topic development phase, have students post their topic (or competing topic) idea(s) to a discussion board forum and require that each student provide a certain number of classmates with helpful feedback on their posted topic. Final paper topics could be due a few days after this activity is completed.

○ During the outline or rough draft phase, create partners or small groups in which students assist one another through this process. Once a full outline or rough draft is complete, require each student within the assigned groups to provide the other students within that group with helpful feedback. Encourage the small groups to continue to talk and work together throughout the remainder of the time they have to finish the final paper.

■ An entire week of an online class could be dedicated to this activity to allow students the time needed to review and critique each other's drafts.

RESOURCES Examples of amicus curiae briefs on issues such as abortion, civil commitment, and the death penalty, among many others, submitted by the American Psychological Association can be found at http://www.apa.org/about/offices/ogc/amicus/index-issues.aspx.

Kearney, J. D., & Merrill, T. W. (2000). The influence of amicus curiae briefs on the Supreme Court. *University of Pennsylvania Law Review, 148*, 743–855. http://dx.doi.org/10.2307/3312826

REFERENCES Black, H. C., & Nolan, J. R. (2014). *Black's law dictionary* (10th ed.). St. Paul, MN: West. Rules of the Supreme Court of the United States. (2013). Part VII. Practice and Procedure. Rule 37(1). Retrieved from https://www.law.cornell.edu/rules/supct/rule_37

17 WHAT WOULD SCOTUS DO?

Understanding how cases move through the state and federal court systems is an important foundational area of knowledge for psychology and law students. This is particularly relevant, given the importance and weight of Supreme Court of the United States (SCOTUS) decisions on major societal issues. This activity will provide students with an opportunity to learn more about various perspectives taken by the current Supreme Court justices, as well as to act out different roles in an appellate court process. Students will research the perspective of a particular justice and decide a case from the justice's perspective.

LEARNING OBJECTIVES

Students will

(a) gain an overview of the appellate trial process,
(b) recognize each SCOTUS justice and understand how SCOTUS comes to a decision,
(c) compare and contrast different perspectives taken by each SCOTUS justice, and
(d) discuss how SCOTUS decisions affect law and policy.

PREPARATION

Prior Didactic Coverage

- The trial and appeals process
- The different types of courts (trial and appeals)
- SCOTUS process, including, for example,
  - how justices are chosen,
  - how they make decisions,
  - the diversity of justices on the Court,
  - how their decisions affect the law (e.g., checks and balances of other branches, future trials/judge-made decisions, a right becomes constitutional when it is affirmed by SCOTUS decision), and
  - the fact that SCOTUS is the only appellate court whose decisions are binding on all lower courts and jurisdictions.
- Overview of each justice and his or her decision-making trends (see Content Note 17.1)

http://dx.doi.org/10.1037/0000080-018
Activities for Teaching Psychology and Law: A Guide for Instructors, by A. D. Zelechoski, M. Wolbransky, and C. L. Riggs Romaine

■ Depending on when this activity is facilitated, you will need to make sure your list and descriptions of the SCOTUS justices is current. For example, at the time this book was written, there were only eight Supreme Court justices, as the late Justice Scalia's chair had not yet been filled. At the time of publication, SCOTUS comprised the following justices:
1. John Roberts, Jr. (Chief Justice)
2. Anthony Kennedy
3. Clarence Thomas
4. Ruth Bader Ginsburg
5. Stephen Breyer
6. Samuel Anthony Alito, Jr.
7. Sonia Sotomayor
8. Elena Kagan
9. Neil Gorsuch

To confirm who is currently on the Court, as well as informative biographical summaries of each justice, review the SCOTUS website at https://www.supremecourt.gov.

Materials Needed

■ Picture printouts of each justice with brief descriptions (see Content Note 17.1)
■ Handout 17.1: What Would SCOTUS Do? (one for each student)

FACILITATION In this activity, students will decide a case based on the perspective of a particular Supreme Court justice. In the first class session, the activity is described, the current justices reviewed and assigned, and various case or issue options presented. You can choose to use one case (likely a recent interesting and relevant "hot topic") with all students writing their opinion based on this case. Alternatively, every nine students could be assigned a different case to decide. Students can either be assigned a certain justice or choose their own. Each student will work outside of class to "decide the case" based on his or her personal perspective (i.e., the assigned justice's perspective). This will highlight the similarities and differences between the justices, as well as the challenges presented to the Supreme Court as a whole.

Class 1

1. Give an overview of the activity to the class, placing the exercise within the broader context of the trial and appellate process.
2. Explain the hypothetical case (or cases) that the Court will be deciding. Possible hot topic issues include the following:
   ■ allowing children to reside in prison with an incarcerated parent,
   ■ legalization of marijuana,
   ■ gun control policies (e.g., requiring background checks or registration), and
   ■ immigration (e.g., allowing those who arrive by boat to remain but turning away those caught by the Coast Guard before reaching the land).
3. Assign, randomly select, or allow students to choose which justice they will role-play. Alternatively, a fun twist on this activity is to substitute various well-known celebrities for the Supreme Court justices and have students render their opinions

from the perspective of that celebrity (or what is known about that celebrity's views or experiences).

Outside of class, students need to do the following:

1. Carefully research their assigned justices, including their age, where they were raised, their work history, and so on, keeping in mind any and all of this information could influence their perspective. Students may find it helpful to look at the justice's previous rulings in similar cases. Information on each justice's perspective and history of decisions is readily available online. Students may find the SCOTUS website (Supreme Court of the United States, n.d.), *Encyclopedia Britannica* ("Supreme Court of the United States," 2016), Wikipedia, or other encyclopedia-type resources helpful for an overall perspective.
2. Write a one-paragraph "ruling" on the case. This should include their final decision (whether to uphold or overrule the lower court decision) and a brief explanation of why and how they came to that decision.

Class 2

1. Bring pictures of each justice and tape them to the board.
2. Begin class by having each group of students assigned to a particular justice share what they learned about him or her. Make some notes on the whiteboard or blackboard under each justice's picture based on the information students provide. This will give the rest of the class the opportunity to learn about the other justices on the Court.
3. Have each student announce his or her ruling to the rest of the class.
4. Tally the rulings and see what the final SCOTUS ruling would be for each assigned case.
5. Discuss these final rulings in more depth:
   a. How did each justice come to his or her decision based on his or her specific background and perspective?
   b. How might the Court write up the final decision (e.g., highlight the differences between a majority, minority, and dissenting opinion)?
   c. What were some of the notable differences between the justices?
   d. How did some justices come to the same conclusion but for different reasons (and how does this affect the Court's overall final decision in a case)?
   e. How might these opinions be used in future cases?
   f. How might they affect law or policy?

DEBRIEFING   At the end of the activity, facilitate a debriefing discussion with students.

Sample Discussion Questions

- How did this exercise affect your understanding of SCOTUS?
- What were the challenges of deciding the case at hand?
- What are your thoughts on how justices are selected?

- What are your thoughts on how long they stay on the bench?
- Do you think this process is an effective means of democratic lawmaking?
- Were any of your personal views affected by this exercise?

GRADING

Grading should be based on each student's participation and engagement in the activity and his or her use of the available information. Appendix B: Participation Grading Rubric can be used or modified for this activity.

Alternatively, or in addition, the one-paragraph write-up can be included as a graded component of the activity and Appendix A: Written Assignment Grading Rubric modified as appropriate. For example, the grading rubric could include the following elements:

- student submitted the write-up based on his or her assigned justice;
- write-up exhibited evidence of justice's background and legal perspective (e.g., more liberal or conservative decision-making history);
- write-up came to a decision on assigned case;
- write-up was well written, absent of grammatical errors and typos;
- student was respectful of peers' views;
- student actively and thoughtfully discussed his or her decision with the class; and/or
- student exhibited understanding of SCOTUS decision-making by actively engaging in the classroom discussion (e.g., offered perspective, asked and answered questions).

MODIFICATIONS

Varying Class Lengths

- If less time is available, have all students decide the same case. This will decrease the amount of time needed to cover each case during the second day. If this method is chosen, have students acting as the same justices compare their decisions with one another and discuss how each came to their decision (especially if they came to different conclusions acting as the same justice).

Varying Class Sizes

- Depending on the class size, all students could be assigned to decide the same or different cases (repeating justices as needed).

Online and/or Hybrid Courses

- Use the same method as already described, but have students write a longer opinion paper. Have students post these opinions for each other to see. Use these posted individual opinions to put together each Court's "final opinion" and post them for students to review. Then engage students in a discussion similar to the format described for an in-person classroom.

REFERENCES

Supreme Court of the United States. (2016). *Encyclopedia Britannica.* Retrieved from https://www.britannica.com/topic/Supreme-Court-of-the-United-States
Supreme Court of the United States. (n.d.). *Biographies of current justices of the Supreme Court.* Retrieved from https://www.supremecourt.gov/about/biographies.aspx

Appendix A

Written Assignment Grading Rubric

Name: Date:

	Description	Total points possible	Points earned
Format	Appropriately formatted, using templates available for the assignment, including appropriate headers and relevant sections		
Argument/content	Includes relevant information Thorough coverage of the assigned topic and appropriate use of argument and examples to support a clear argument, thesis, or objective		
Writing	Free of errors Clear writing style appropriate for the assignment and intended audience		
Citations/references	Resources and references are appropriately cited in text and in American Psychological Association Style		
Assignment requirements	Meets assigned requirements for length, content, topic coverage, etc.		
Final score			

Feedback/Explanation:

Appendix B

Participation Grading Rubric

Name: Date:

Activity:

	Description	Total points possible	Student's score
Attended class activity	Attended entire class, on the day(s) activity was scheduled		
Came to class prepared	Came to class with necessary work completed Exhibited knowledge of previous readings/videos assigned Submitted assignments on time		
Engaged in topical discussion	Participated throughout the entire classroom activity by offering relevant comments, ideas, and/or feedback to others Exhibited knowledge of related class topic Discussion was meaningful, substantive, and moved the conversation forward		
Demonstrated classroom etiquette	Exhibited respect throughout class by listening to classmates Refrained from speaking out of turn or having side conversations Did not engage in other distracting behavior		
Worked well in small group	Engaged in small-group discussions with classmates, as assigned Showed respect to group ideas Offered meaningful contributions to small group work		

Total Score: _____/_____

Feedback/Explanation:

Appendix C

Presentation Grading Rubric

Group Members: Date:

Title/Description of Project Presented:

	Points possible	Points received	Comments
Effective utilization of group members (*if applicable*)			
Effective use of time			
Content and ideas			
Organization			
Creativity and innovation			
Integration and application of themes and content from the class			
Total			

Feedback/Explanation:

Appendix D

Group and Self-Evaluation Form

Name: _____ Date: _____

Activity Name: _____

Instructions: Write group members' names across the top row in the numbered boxes. Assign a value for each characteristic listed for both yourself and each group member.

1: *Strongly disagree*   2: *Disagree*   3: *Neutral*   4: *Agree*   5: *Strongly agree*

	You	1.	2.	3.	4.	5.
Contributed ideas						
Listened to and respected others' ideas						
Cooperated with other members						
Took initiative						
Prepared for group meetings						
Communicated effectively with teammates						
Completed work on time						
Contributed meaningfully including his/her designated material						
Column total:						
Percentage of the final product this group member contributed*						

*Allocate a total of 100% points among your group with higher percentages going to those members who contributed the most. In the case of equal contributions, points should be divided equally among team members.

Optional open-ended questions:

My greatest strengths as a team member were:

The group work skills I could improve are:

What I enjoyed most about this group project:

What I enjoyed the least about this group project:

Appendix E

Sample Activity Feedback Survey

Activity: Who Do You Want? The *Voir Dire* Process

Your name (optional): _____

Please circle the number that best represents your answer.

1. I was nervous or anxious about participating in this activity.

1	2	3	4	5
Strongly Disagree		Somewhat Agree		Strongly Agree

2. The jury selection activity helped me to understand the class material better.

1	2	3	4	5
Strongly Disagree		Somewhat Agree		Strongly Agree

3. The jury selection activity was a good supplement to the lecture on this topic.

1	2	3	4	5
Strongly Disagree		Somewhat Agree		Strongly Agree

4. The jury selection activity helped me understand the jury selection process.

1	2	3	4	5
Strongly Disagree		Somewhat Agree		Strongly Agree

5. The jury selection activity helped me understand the difference between challenges for cause and peremptory challenges.

1	2	3	4	5
Strongly Disagree		Somewhat Agree		Strongly Agree

6. The jury selection activity helped me understand the jury selection requirements, including using the *Batson*-type challenge.

1	2	3	4	5
Strongly Disagree		Somewhat Agree		Strongly Agree

7. To what extent would you recommend the jury selection activity in a psychology and law course?

1	2	3	4	5
Do Not Recommend at All		Somewhat Recommend		Strongly Recommend

8. How willing would you be to participate in the jury selection activity again?

1	2	3	4	5
Extremely Unwilling		Somewhat Willing		Extremely Willing

9. My questions and needs were adequately addressed before my participation in the activity.

1	2	3	4	5
Strongly Disagree		Somewhat Agree		Strongly Agree

10. The handouts provided before I participated in the activity were helpful.

1	2	3	4	5
Strongly Disagree		Somewhat Agree		Strongly Agree

11. The process and components of this activity were clearly laid out, and I had a good understanding of what was expected of me going into the activity.

1	2	3	4	5
Strongly Disagree		Somewhat Agree		Strongly Agree

12. I enjoyed participating in this activity.

1	2	3	4	5
Strongly Disagree		Somewhat Agree		Strongly Agree

13. This activity was a good way to learn about jury selection.

1	2	3	4	5
Strongly Disagree		Somewhat Agree		Strongly Agree

14. Because of my participation in this activity, I think I have a better understanding of jury selection than other concepts I have learned in this class.

1	2	3	4	5
Strongly Disagree		Somewhat Agree		Strongly Agree

Overall impression of the activity:

Comments and suggestions for improving the activity:

INDEX

ABOUT THE AUTHORS

Amanda D. Zelechoski, JD, PhD, ABPP, is an associate professor of psychology at Valparaiso University, where she primarily teaches courses in psychology and law, child and adolescent psychopathology, professional development in psychology, psychotherapy and counseling, and Inside-Out prison exchange courses. She is a licensed clinical and forensic psychologist and attorney, as well as a risk management consultant for The Trust. In addition to best practices in teaching and training in psychology and law, her research focuses on the intersection of psychology, law, and trauma, particularly related to forensic and mental health assessment, delinquency, and child custody and welfare. Dr. Zelechoski received her BA from the University of Notre Dame, her MS and PhD from Drexel University, and her JD from Villanova University School of Law. She completed a postdoctoral fellowship at the Trauma Center at Justice Resource Institute (Brookline, MA) and is board certified in clinical child and adolescent psychology. She received the 2016 American Psychology–Law Society Early Career Outstanding Teaching and Mentoring Award and the 2014 Valparaiso University Arts & Sciences Emerging Teacher Award.

Melinda Wolbransky, JD, PhD, is a licensed attorney and clinical and forensic psychologist in Los Angeles, California, where she is the evaluation manager for Gateways Hospital and Mental Health Center's Conditional Release Program, providing psychological evaluations, expert witness testimony, and court liaison services for Los Angeles and San Diego counties. She has taught various psychology and law, general psychology, and criminal justice classes at several universities, including John Jay College of Criminal Justice, Drexel University, and the University of New Haven. She specializes in online teaching formats, having spent the past 4 years modifying course content and related experiential activities to an online setting. In addition to conducting research on effective ways to teach psychology and law, she also looks at how jury decision-making (particularly those in capital cases) is affected by evidence related to the defendant's mental illness. Dr. Wolbransky received her BS, MS, and PhD from Drexel University and her JD from Villanova University School of Law. In her free time, she enjoys traveling, running, and making the most of the California sunshine.

Christina L. Riggs Romaine, PhD, is an assistant professor of psychology at Wheaton College, where she teaches courses in psychology and law, child psychopathology, and research methodology. She is a licensed clinical psychologist and associate with the National Youth Screening and Assessment Partners, providing training to juvenile justice stakeholders on implementation of evidence-based risk assessment and practices. In addition to best practices in teaching and training in law and psychology, her research focuses on the juvenile justice system and youth's understanding and appreciation of rights, as well as factors influencing their risk-taking decisions. Dr. Riggs Romaine received her BA from Gordon College and her MS and PhD from Drexel University. She completed her postdoctoral fellowship in forensic psychology at the University of Massachusetts Medical School. Before joining academia, she was a full-time clinician in the Essex County Juvenile Court Clinic, where she provided forensic mental health evaluations for the court and served as an expert witness.

Melinda Wolbransky, Christina L. Riggs Romaine, and Amanda D. Zelechoski